Lisa Millar is the co-host of ABC TV's *News Breakfast*. She returned to the ABC in Australia after finishing a decade-long posting as bureau chief in both London and Washington DC, covering some of the world's biggest stories. Lisa began her career at the *Gympie Times* in 1988 and has worked in print, TV and radio. She won a Walkley Award in 2005 for investigative reporting.

Lisa narrated the hugely popular ABC TV series *Muster Dogs* and is the author of a bestselling memoir *Daring to Fly*.

Muster Dogs series one and two were produced by Ambience Entertainment in 2021 and 2023.

AMBIENCE

To My Dear Dear Sister
Viy

Lisa Millar

MUSTER DOGS

FROM PUPS TO PROS

How ten dogs stole hearts
and changed lives

Merry Christmas 2024

ABC
BOOKS

Photos of Aticia Grey, CJ Scotney, Joni Hall and Rob Tuncks on page viii by Steve Strike
Photo of Frank Finger on page viii by Lisa Millar
Photos of Lily Davies-Etheridge and Russ Fowler on page ix by Ben Emery
Photos of Cilla Pershouse and Zoe Miller on page ix by Monica O'Brien
Photo of Steve Elliott on page ix by Melissa Spencer

 The ABC 'Wave' device is a trademark of the
Australian Broadcasting Corporation and is used
under licence by HarperCollins*Publishers* Australia.

HarperCollins*Publishers*
Australia • Brazil • Canada • France • Germany • Holland • India
Italy • Japan • Mexico • New Zealand • Poland • Spain • Sweden
Switzerland • United Kingdom • United States of America

HarperCollins acknowledges the Traditional Custodians
of the land upon which we live and work, and pays respect
to Elders past and present.

First published on Gadigal Country in Australia in 2024
by HarperCollins*Publishers* Australia Pty Limited
ABN 36 009 913 517
harpercollins.com.au

A catalogue record for this book is available from the National Library of Australia.

ISBN 978 0 7333 4309 4 (paperback)
ISBN 978 1 4607 1665 6 (ebook)

Cover design by HarperCollins Design Studio
Front cover image of Lisa Millar by Jesse Smith
Back cover image of Zoe Miller and her dog Buddy by Melissa Spencer, Stock Chick Films
Photo of Lisa Millar on page i by Jesse Smith
Typeset in Sabon LT Std by Kirby Jones
Printed and bound in Australia by McPherson's Printing Group

This book was written on the lands of the Kulin nation.

Series one and two of Muster Dogs were filmed and produced on the lands of the Bungandidj, Djab Wurrung, Gunditjmara, Jardwadjali, Jupagulk, Koa, Miriwoong, Barkandji, Wagiman, Wakka Wakka, Wergaia, Wiradjuri, Wotjobaluk and Yinggarda peoples.

To the wonderful Muster Dogs *participants,*
who let us into their lives and taught us about
respect and kindness.

SERIES ONE

Frank Finger with Annie (left) and Luci (formally Lucifer, right)

CJ Scotney with Spice

Joni Hall with Chet

Rob Tuncks with Lucifer

Aticia Grey with Gossip

SERIES TWO

Zoe Miller with Buddy

Cilla Pershouse with Ash Barky

Russ Fowler with Molly

Lily Davies-Etheridge with Snow

Steve Elliott with Indi

Contents

PROLOGUE

It was 'brush your teeth and get into your pyjamas time' on a hot Sunday night across Australia. People had finished dinner and were jamming plates into already overpacked dishwashers. Some had bowls of ice cream balanced on their knees while their friends searched for the remote control or began streaming on devices.

It was 23 January 2022, the dying days of another summer break. The holidays had been shadowed by uncertainty and loss – lost families, lost friends, lost jobs. Borders had been shut then opened, masks were still attached resolutely to some faces, while others had long been discarded by owners rebelling against the rules that had dictated their lives for the previous two years.

But all of that was to be forgotten for 60 magical minutes. The first episode of *Muster Dogs* was about to drop.

It had been an experiment on every level, an ambitious idea to give five adorable livestock-herding kelpie pups to graziers and trainers around Australia to see if nature or nurture would determine if they could become champion working dogs. Instead of the normal three years of training, each pup would be given just 12 months, the tightest of schedules.

Filmmakers Monica O'Brien and Michael Boughen were on edge. Nothing about this project had been easy. They had dealt with funding uncertainties, border closures, Covid sickness, camera-shy farmers and, of course, a litter of eight-week-old pups, who quickly became bundles of mischief, captivating everyone while they tried to run amok.

Now all their efforts rested on a first night TV premiere.

Monica's sister had baked what she hoped would be a celebratory cake – a farm paddock topped with toy cattle and shredded coconut for hay. Two plastic dogs plonked into the thick chocolate icing appeared to be sliding down the edge of the sponge, ready to topple off with one quick kick from a cow.

Monica texted me a photo of the cake and I replied, 'Wonderful!!' But those perilously positioned dogs struck me as a metaphor for what everyone had endured. All they – and we – could do was hang on tight.

'This show is going to be bloody brilliant,' I added,

summoning confidence I didn't feel and using all the emojis I could find in a hurry.

As the minutes ticked down towards the broadcast, Monica sent me another text: 'I'm afraid it won't live up to the hype.'

And the hype was real: the previews in the papers and online had been promising big things. But the slightly irregular timeslot of 7.40pm threatened to be yet another hurdle. During the pandemic, the Sunday evening ABC news had been extended by ten minutes and there must have been a temptation for viewers to find their regular 7.30pm Sunday blockbusters elsewhere. It felt to us on the *Muster Dogs* team that the ABC had been promoting the show on a continuous loop to avoid just that.

In *The Weekend Australian* the day before, Graeme Blundell encouraged people to tune in, writing that '*Muster Dogs* is simply delightful TV as well as being thoughtful, engaged and cast with a bunch of wonderful characters.'

Those characters – the participants in series one: Frank, CJ, Joni, Rob and Aticia – also had mixed feelings that night. None had been in the national spotlight before. They were people of the land – hardworking, no-nonsense graziers and dog owners – who'd privately at times wondered why on earth they'd signed up to do the show in the first place. They'd been plucked from their already busy lives and given a duty of care for a valuable animal, and now all of Australia would see whether they'd been up to the task.

On his property in Clermont, Queensland, Frank Finger enjoyed the last of the brisket that had been cooking in the smoker for the previous ten hours. It had been rubbed with a mix of spices and had sat marinating for another 12 hours before that. As the clock ticked towards 7.40pm, Frank, the oldest of the participants at 68, sat down with a glass of red wine and patiently waited. He hadn't seen any of the early edited material. 'Nothing at all, I didn't know what to expect,' he recalled later.

But he wasn't nervous. He trusted the filmmakers. His grandchildren sprawled on the loungeroom floor in front of the brand-new television, with its huge screen, bought especially for the occasion. 'The other one was on its last legs, so I thought why not?' There were about 18 family and friends in the room that night but not one word was spoken until the final credits rolled.

Up north, CJ Scotney, who'd juggled a family and the demands of her property in the Northern Territory for the nine months it took to produce the series, sat down to watch with her sister and her family, who were visiting from South Australia, only to be thwarted by a wild tropical storm that took out the satellite television. An hour later, after a leisurely dinner, they started again, trying to ignore the phone calls coming in from friends who'd already watched the whole episode.

In Victoria, Rob Tuncks, whose dog Lucifer would steal viewers' hearts, settled in to watch the tennis instead. He'd been pretty chilled throughout the long filming process and his demeanour on broadcast night was no different. Besides, it was round four of the Australian Open in Melbourne and Ash Barty was under pressure from opponent Amanda Anisimova. The temperature on Rod Laver Arena was sitting stubbornly around 30 degrees. And on court the tension was palpable. Anisimova broke Barty's 63-game serving streak.

Australian tennis fans were holding their collective breath. And so were the ABC producers who'd been through the wringer to get their new TV show across the line. They knew the first episode of the *Muster Dogs* experiment would be up against the always high-rating tennis, but the Queen of Australian tennis, Ash Barty, herself? That was a blow. And if one of the *Muster Dogs* participants was choosing to watch the tennis over the show he was starring in, would the rest of the nation do the same?

Joni Hall was visiting friends in Perth. They'd ordered pizza and she tucked into a cheese platter as she watched herself on television. She'd been reticent about opening up her life and exposing herself in this very public way. The beers helped to calm her nerves that night.

Further north in Western Australia, Aticia Grey was out on her property, caught up with late cattle work. With an eye on the clock, she knew she was never going to make it back in time. She was glad she'd thought to record the episode through their satellite television service.

Dog trainers Neil and Helen McDonald, whose expertise was central to the program, had just finished teaching a three-day dog school at their property in Keith in the southeast corner of South Australia. That evening, they set up a TV screen on the grass in front of their shearing shed and dragged old couches outside. As 7.40pm approached, they opened beers for the dozen or so students who'd travelled long distances to study their training techniques and sat down to watch. They were nervous. But they couldn't get the technology to work in time for the broadcast so they had to stream it later that night on ABC iview. They binged until 3am, watching all four episodes and turning a critical eye over everything they'd done in front of the cameras, immediately wishing some words and actions had been edited out and others left in.

I sat alone in my Melbourne apartment. I'd cooked a chicken stir-fry earlier that evening, cleaned up the soy sauce splatter and put the leftovers in the fridge. Early dinners were part of my routine. I'd been co-hosting ABC *News Breakfast* for two and half years in the South Melbourne studios and the pattern of my week was locked in. I'd go to bed shortly after 8pm, put my alarm on for 3am, and be out the door at 3.30am, ready for the three hours of live television. It was a regimen that was guaranteed to make most people grimace. But tonight the routine would be broken.

The show was broken into four episodes, each about an hour long, and I knew every word of the 140-page script. I'd recorded the narration over a period of nine stressful weeks, when the pressure on everyone involved in the project was at its peak. I'd seen rough cuts and spent hours on the phone and on Zoom with the filmmakers and ABC producers. Now I needed to see and listen to it 'in real life'. I flopped into an armchair and texted my brothers and sisters and their families to remind them the show was about to start.

I smiled, remembering that when I'd first told friends about this project they thought I was working on a show called 'Mustard Dogs'. 'Whaaat?' someone had asked, their face crinkling. 'Like hot dogs but animals?'

Other friends misheard it as 'Master Dogs' and assumed it was a spinoff of a *MasterChef* reality show. It was neither of those. It was the work of a handful of people on the leanest of budgets who were about to realise a dream that had been five years in the making.

How had they managed to pull off filming more than 300 hours of footage across the country for an observational documentary at a moment in history when most people weren't even leaving their homes?

Monica, who'd juggled two young children during the show's production, sat at her dining room table near the cake her sister had made. She had seen the show 'a billion times' and was more interested in watching the reactions of a friend and his teenage sons who were all squished onto a four-seater couch. She sent one more text to her close friend and colleague Sally Browning. They are words that would resonate with women around the world: 'What if they find out I'm an imposter?'

'Yeah that, or everyone realises you're a genius,' Sally responded.

It was time.

At 7.40pm, a gently played piano provided the soundtrack to the opening scenes – sweeping drone footage over the rich green grass of a sheep farm in the Grampian Mountain range of Victoria. And then the real stars of this show finally had their moment. A litter of tiny black and red kelpies appeared on screen, wriggling and squirming, making soft little grunts as they searched for the comfort of their mother.

Within half an hour, social media platforms were filled with posts from people responding in real time, sensing they were witnessing something magical. Viewers posted videos of their own dogs barking in encouragement as they watched the show, and urged people to switch over to the ABC.

But it wouldn't be until the next morning that the *Muster Dogs* team would truly understand what had transpired. The daily overnight ratings report is released at 8.30am and, as it hits the inboxes of executives and reviewers across Australia, the narrative about a show's success or failure begins to be written. The ratings system is considered by some to be an outdated way to judge television-viewing habits in a world where streaming prevails. But in TV world it still matters.

Jo Chichester, who was then the manager of ABC Screen, had discussed with colleagues what ratings would be considered a 'best-case scenario'. A show in the same timeslot the previous year had rated around 700,000. With the competition facing them that night they knew it was all guesswork.

Muster Dogs attracted nearly 1.5 million viewers in the citics and regional areas on that first night. These are huge numbers in the Australian market where anything over 800,000 is big.

Filmmaker Michael Boughen had watched the episode with his wife at home in regional Victoria. Michael's friend at a commercial network texted him first with the news. 'It's a hit,' he wrote.

And so it was. Within a year *Muster Dogs* had been watched many millions of times and was the number-one rating non-kids show for the ABC in 2022. The overall number-one was another show about dogs: the internationally adored *Bluey*. Pet owners around Australia were whispering, 'Lovely dog, lovely dog,' to their animals, mimicking Frank Finger's calm ways with his winning kelpie, Annie.

The show had won hearts all over the world – children, adults and dogs alike. This is the story of why a television program about working dogs and their trainers became a phenomenon, and why we care so much about the heartfelt messages it delivered.

Indi finding her confidence with sheep twice her size. (Melissa Spencer)

CHAPTER 1

Taking the Gamble

Pinpointing a beginning can be complicated but the origin of *Muster Dogs* goes back to a birthday party in regional Victoria. Michael Boughen, a filmmaker who up to that point had concentrated on feature-length movies, suggested to his partner, Fiona, that they leave the city and move to the bush.

It was well before Covid turned the world upside down. Michael and Fiona already had a country property, but they weren't happy with its location, so they bought another one and decided to just 'up stakes and go'. We'd all heard of a sea-change, but Michael and Fiona were the first of a big wave of green-changers that became a tidal wave of movement during the pandemic.

Michael had grown up on a farm, but he'd lost sight of the relationship he'd had with the land and the animals as he wound up in big films, big TV and big cities. Their new property was close to Bendigo, and Michael's plan was to travel to Sydney weekly using a newly opened airport just ten minutes away. His sister lived nearby and it was during her seventieth birthday party on her farm in April 2018 that the idea took shape.

'There was a bunch of puppies there,' Michael recalls, 'and they were wheeling them out: "OK, OK, who wants a puppy?"' I was looking at them, thinking, *God, they're so cute, so gorgeous.'*

He didn't go home with a puppy that day but he did go home with an idea. Ideas in TV often take a long time to come to anything, if at all, with many going no further than a few notes in an email. They need drive, timing and luck. This one was no different. Michael felt there was something about those animals that would make good television, but what? He knew that gorgeous pups became incredibly efficient working dogs if bred and trained properly. And it became clear from subsequent conversations with neighbours and friends that no matter how many choppers, bikes and horses a grazier had, if they didn't have a muster dog, life would be tough.

He had a lot of questions. When you're a brand-new farmer, what do you do? How do you find a dog? How do you train a dog?

There was one bloke who everyone seemed to respect – South Australian trainer Neil McDonald. If you signed up for one of Neil's dog schools, then chances were you'd be able to train your pup into a valuable working dog. But starting with a good quality pup was critical to the equation. And as Michael dug deeper, a couple of names kept popping up – Joc Spicer in Victoria and Peter Barr in South Australian.

Michael's idea started taking shape.

The television scene in Australia is small compared to the international markets, and local production companies and creatives are in a constant flow of pitching ideas and hoping something will get picked up while they're working on the next project. On a Monday morning in 2018, in the office of Ambience Entertainment on the north shore of Sydney, Michael sat down with producers Monica O'Brien and Sally Browning. They pulled together a pitch for a show they'd already tentatively called 'Muster Dogs' and took it to the ABC at its Ultimo headquarters in Sydney, where they met with Jo Chichester in the foyer near the café.

It may be an urban myth but the higher up the food chain you are in the creative world in Australia, the higher up the building your meetings take place. The foyer was not the most encouraging start, but at least they had an ABC executive in front of them – and not just any executive but Jo Chichester, a commissioning editor. Jo thought their idea had legs and suggested making it into some sort of competition. Not a nasty, backbiting 'win at all costs' kind of reality show, but one with a feel-good, family-orientated 'we're all in this together' vibe. It would be another 18 months before the show had enough backing to get underway.

They needed participants from different parts of Australia, who would be able to give an insight into different aspects of life on the land. They settled on five because they wanted to avoid an even number of participants and it would be a good spread of storylines across four episodes. Dog trainer Neil McDonald offered to reach out to people who he knew cared about the industry and their animals as much as he did. He thought of himself as something of a talent scout and had no idea he would end up playing such a crucial role in the show.

Participant Rob Tuncks joined early. He was confident the filmmakers' ethics and values aligned with his. It had been 15 years since Rob had walked away from a successful corporate career as a stockbroker to pursue his real passion: to live off the land. And after spending the first stint of his new life using motorbikes to muster sheep, his patience and understanding of working dogs had grown. He'd become a true believer in the importance of dogs in mustering livestock and he wanted to share that with the rest of Australia.

He took a gamble taking part in the show and became something of a comic-relief character at times during the filming, with his cartoonish baseball cap in stark contrast to the wide-brimmed brown traditional hats preferred by people on the land. One of Rob's most memorable scenes featured him chasing his kelpie, Lucifer, around the yard calling out, 'Come here, you little bastard!' His laugh leapt out of the screen. And we laughed with him. But little did we know then that Rob was taking part for an important reason and that without him we might not have come to know Frank and Joni, CJ and Aticia.

'Most people in the rural industry are very scared of media coming in and filming stuff and [think] they always show the worst thing – for example, if something bad happened in the yards,' Rob told me later. 'Even with the best operators it happens; every now and then you lose an animal, or it injures itself and has to be put down. But I felt we could trust these guys.'

With Rob in their corner, Michael and Monica, who had worked together producing television and films since 2007, had their first grazier. They had a trainer in Neil as well as some possible participants who were considering the pitch.

Frank Finger was a cattleman Neil had his eye on. Frank would give the show a different landscape in Queensland from Rob in Victoria and, given he was in his late sixties, he would also be a different generation to Rob. Perhaps *Muster Dogs* was a story about generational change as well?

Frank's introduction to working dogs is quite a story. He left school at 15 and worked driving trucks at a coal mine before returning to the family farm in Clermont in central

Queensland. He had no idea what farm dogs could do until he was helping train young students at agricultural college and was asked if he could organise a dog school. This was back in 1996. Frank hunted around and learned that Neil McDonald and his wife, Helen, a fellow dog trainer, would come up to Queensland. So he organised to have 380 fresh weaners in the yard, thinking they'd be needed for the dog school. It took Frank and his family about a week on horseback to round up all those young cattle and get them in the yard, and as Neil and Helen prepped nearby for the next day's dog school, Frank and his daughters put their horses and saddles away.

'Then I looked up and a gate had swung open, and 380 weaners were streaming out back towards the hills where they'd come from,' Frank remembered, still feeling the despair of that moment. 'I said to Neil, "I'll have to grab the horses." But Neil looked up and said, "Oh, Helen will take care of that."

'So Helen walked over to the trailer and let out an old dog called Dudley and another dog called Tina. Helen sent one dog to the right and one to the left and, even though the cattle were now more than half a kilometre away, those two dogs were enough to get the herd back. Helen didn't utter a word, there were no commands, and it was as if the cattle were searching for her, and I have never seen anything like it. Right from that very first moment I knew I wanted to do it because I could see that one person could do so much.'

Frank still thinks he'll never be as good as Helen, but he'll keep trying. His whole family took on dogs, and Neil's schools became a regular event at their property. Now, he says, he feels like he's forgotten to get dressed if he heads out into the paddock without a dog.

Frank might love dogs, but he also loves cattle. He has a connection to them. He enjoys seeing the life cycle begin and the calves fattening up on the land. He does it, he says, because he has a sense of responsibility to help feed the nation. Frank loves music too. Anything from Rod Stewart to Shania Twain to Robbie Williams and the Bee Gees. He listens to it when he's eating, when he gets up in the morning, when he's mustering. But the best music, he says, is rain on a tin roof. 'There's nothing sweeter than that. I can sing to it.'

He doesn't always take all his dogs with him on his long days of mustering. The dogs that stay behind get to listen to a radio that he keeps on in their kennels. One of Frank's favourites is an old song that Willie Nelson released to mark his eighty-seventh birthday. There's a line in the song where Willie sings of keeping your friends close and toasting every sunset with a drink. 'That's what we try to do,' says Frank. 'We might do that tonight.'

All of the participants in series one gave us a laugh at different times, even if it was unintentional. CJ, in the Northern Territory, took on the training of her muster dogs with a lot of seriousness. She dedicated her spare time to getting her kelpie puppy, Spice, up to scratch, so we had a laugh when she discovered her husband, Joe, and nine-year-old daughter, Lindsay, had snuck off on a fishing trip without her.

CJ and Joe bought their property determined to also have a good lifestyle. 'So I encourage Joe that if he wants to go fishing then he should go do that and I'll stay home; and then while I go camp drafting he's happy to stay home,' she explains. Camp drafting involves a horse rider corralling cattle in a yard, and then separating one from the pack and showing off the rider's skills by keeping the beast under control. It was a hobby CJ was passionate about.

The property they own is known as Garabaldi, a First Nations name for one of the hills on the land. CJ's a descendant of the Wagadagam people from Mabuyag Island in the Torres Strait. She and Joe have been in the Douglas Daly region, about 250 kilometres south of Darwin, for almost 15 years. They run their property without any other staff, unless you count their working dogs, which number around seven.

CJ comes from a big family, so she grew up surrounded by people. The youngest of six girls, she spent school holidays and weekends fencing and working the cattle, preparing the paddocks. 'There was plenty of fun stuff too – cubby houses, exploring World War II ruins. Grandpa taught me about the bush, the stars and to respect all animals.' She told me this in a text message, which can be the best way to communicate with someone often out of range and running a remote cattle property.

Cattle farming goes back many generations in CJ's family, starting with her great-grandfather on her mother's side. She wanted to take part in *Muster Dogs* to honour that legacy but, more so, to have a chance to tell Australians about the pride she has in the agricultural industry and the advances being made.

Aticia Grey also comes from a long line of cattle farmers and is passionate about working with dogs, but it took her a bit more convincing to join the show. Neil McDonald met Aticia when she'd attended one of his dog schools in Western Australia and he thought she'd be perfect for the series. But it wasn't a great time for Aticia.

She was running Glenflorrie Station in the southwest Pilbara of Western Australia with her partner, Adam, and her mum, Susan. They'd had to send almost all of their cattle away, destocking their property after four years of drought. They knew the cattle wouldn't be back until there'd been some decent rain and only after the country had had a chance to recover. It was the most extreme drought they'd seen, and Aticia's family had been on that property since 1992. Even going back over the records to the early 1900s they couldn't find a time that had been that bad. It was rough hilly country that stretched out for over 200,000 hectares and they'd been running Brahmans, which were in high demand for the export market. The weather had always been the hardest thing to deal with for Aticia and her family.

The first time the producers approached Aticia to take part in *Muster Dogs,* she was in the thick of destocking and things looked grim. She didn't have the time or the mental capacity to take on a puppy and try to train it in one year rather than the usual three. The show wasn't ready to film anyway and so nothing more was said. But then sometime later, the producers tried again – and this time Aticia said yes. They were still in the middle of the drought, but the cattle were gone and she could dedicate time to the project.

'I love the idea of showcasing the working dog and highlighting how valuable they can be,' she said when asked on camera why she wanted to be involved in the show. 'They've all got their personalities and their characters and their quirks, and they deserve to be more than just a tool because they work their hearts out for you if you give them a chance and they don't ask for much in return at all. You take a three-month-old, four-month-old, even six-month-old pup out [into the yards] and you watch that light bulb turn on and they just love it when you put them out on stock and that natural instinct comes through.'

Filming with Aticia was possibly the hardest challenge for the crew. First of all, there was the complication of Covid and closed borders. Then there was the stock issue: she'd kept a handful of stock for her team dogs because, even without the show, she needed to let the dogs feel they were still 'working'. It's in their DNA and they don't just take a few months off because the place is destocked. And then there was the simple fact that she lives a long way from anywhere. Viewers of the program were stunned to learn her driveway is 88 kilometres long. It takes an hour and a half of driving on dirt just to get to the bitumen. When I caught up with her after the series had gone to air, she was still chuckling that people were so shocked by that fact.

'A lot of it seems normal for me because I grew up with it,' she said. 'Because of our driveway, we don't get to town very often and we only get our mail once a week, it's dropped at the neighbour's place or our mailbox, which is an hour and a half away.'

There's country living. And then there's living in the country.

'Our store room on the property is basically our own little supermarket and we always have a bit of everything on hand,' Aticia said.

In her words, Aticia stumbled into dogs. She'd had a kelpie as a kid but the dog's work drive was too strong and the family had no idea what to do with her so she was sent to a sheep farm. It was on a visit to New Zealand that Aticia watched working dogs in action and had her interest piqued. Friends encouraged her to attend a dog school run by Neil McDonald and by the end of those few days she was hooked.

Aticia hadn't realised there was something missing in her life until she had the dogs. When she began working with them, there weren't a lot of people in the region using them. The Pilbara is a vast landscape where helicopters, motorbikes and buggies were always considered the best tools. 'There were a lot of people who thought I was pretty mad and even Dad wasn't a huge advocate.' She soon proved them wrong and hoped that taking part in *Muster Dogs* would ram home the added value of using dogs on properties like hers.

Each of our participants was driven by a desire to share knowledge about their industry, especially to a city audience, but the paths that took them to the show were very different.

Most of us have had a life-changing event that has altered our courses unexpectedly. For me, it was a charter flight when I was a young reporter in Townsville. I had been asked to go to a mine in central Queensland to interview the mine manager for a story our colleagues in Brisbane were doing. On the return flight, we hit severe thunderstorms and the pilot weaved his way around the storm cells looking for a clearer flight path.

We were using a lot of fuel, and what should have been the straight line of our flight path to Townsville started looking like a drunk walking home after a big night. The rain was lashing the windows when the pilot switched to the reserve fuel tank. Suddenly the left-side engine stalled and the right one strained to keep us airborne. An airlock had starved the engine of fuel.

The engine restarted within seconds, but the incident kicked off a fear of flying in me that became chronic over the next ten years. I eventually recovered, and the experience was pivotal in making me who I am today. Being able to overcome that fear was empowering and put me on paths I would otherwise not have taken.

Joni Hall's experience in her early twenties almost took her life but it also led her to become one of Australia's great cattlewomen, and consequently a participant in *Muster Dogs*.

As a kid she was always in a rush. A self-confessed 'feral', she grew up with ten cousins on a property near Clermont in central Queensland. Her dad and his two brothers were catapulted into managing it early after the sudden death of their father. They never had a chance to leave the farm and learn from others before becoming fulltime graziers. But Joni's dad sent her to boarding school to make sure she didn't miss out as he had, and she knew that returning to the family property was never going to be a real option.

'There's only twenty years between me and the youngest brother, my uncle, and you could work on a station for your family and think that something might come out of it in the end. But by the time he's ready to retire, I was pretty sure I was going to be ready too,' she says, rationalising the decisions that came next.

She studied agricultural science and got her first job as a stockwoman, earning a reputation for working hard – so hard, her bosses joked, they could wind her up and let her go and she'd keep working until they came to get her. She bounced from one job to another on properties across Queensland, but it was while she was working in a feedlot that Joni first noticed the impact of stress on cattle from machinery or the way they were treated by workers. Stressed and agitated cattle risk harming themselves as well as the people around them. People who work with dogs find that their cattle are way more subdued, which makes the workplace safer and more harmonious.

In 2003, something happened that changed the direction of Joni's life. She was working alone shifting cattle one day on a property about 90 kilometres out from Richmond in North Queensland (about 500 kilometres west of Townsville).

'I used to get really hot-headed really quickly,' she says as a preamble to her story. 'There was one old cow that just did not want to leave the yards. And 'cause I was so hot-headed, I just glazed over. I went to throw her on my four-wheeler bike, and I got too far behind her and I clipped her back leg with the front tyre of the four-wheeler and it spat me clean out to the side. I had a little graze here on my arm and that was all the injury that happened, but the bike then rolled over and landed on my legs. And I was on my own.'

She had a two-way radio but it was swung over the handlebars out of reach. Every now and then she was able to lift the bike just enough to let the blood flow, but she couldn't swing her legs out. Joni lay there for seven hours until she was rescued by her boss, Spud. She spent nine months trying to build the strength to walk again. It was a miracle they didn't amputate.

'I had seven hours to think about it, stuck under the motorbike, to think about my actions. So out of that I learned this: to be patient and it'll just come.'

Ironically, during her rehabilitation, and despite her boss's protests, she still moved cattle by strapping her leg to a crutch and then strapping the crutch to the four-wheel buggy. She discovered it was helping her dog skills because she had to learn a way to work better with the dogs in order to get the job done. Her boss only managed to get her to slow down and recuperate by sending her to work with Neil McDonald at his dog school in South Australia, creating training videos for a few months.

Fast forward 17 years and Joni had become one of the most sought-after cattle educators, teaching young cattle, or weaners, to be self-sufficient on pasture without their mothers, to be compliant and pliable, and to know how to eat and drink and walk through yards.

There was a nice pattern to her life, travelling with her 20 dogs and working for clients across Western Australia, the Northern Territory and Queensland. Then Neil rang to twist her arm to take part in *Muster Dogs*.

*

It had been a couple of years since Michael had latched on to the idea of a show featuring dogs, after seeing the puppies at his sister's place. The characters for this first series were starting to fall into place even if the show's structure was still embryonic. *Muster Dogs* would be an experiment: to see if what made up the legend of the Australian working dog was brought about by nature or by nurture. It would pose the question of whether you could train a puppy to become a muster dog over the course of a year, instead of the usual industry-standard of three years. By speeding up the training, could dogs could be put to work earlier and become valuable members of the team sooner?

But you can't make a show about dogs without puppies, and all the production plans in the world can't dictate how successfully a dog might mate. The producers asked breeder Joe Spicer if he could deliver half a dozen puppies that could be given to graziers around Australia, and as a backup Peter Barr was enlisted to see what he could produce. 'I've always been big on having insurance and having options,' Michael said.

After years of waiting, things were now moving fast. The production schedule was set and, with dog pregnancies lasting an average of two months, Joe was under pressure to deliver a litter in circumstances that were foreign to him. Ordinarily if someone asked him for a pup, he would have plenty of questions: 'What's the prospective owner's personality? What sort of work do they want the dog doing, is it sheep or cattle? Is it northern country or open country? Is it high rainfall? Or smaller, more-intense farming?' But he wanted to be involved in the show to promote Australia's working dogs, so he got to work finding a love match.

And then came a blow none of them were anticipating – a global pandemic that was shutting down the world. TV shows were put into hibernation and production teams dismantled. But *Muster Dogs* producer Monica O'Brien refused to be bowed. She told the ABC they could still deliver.

'I rang them and said, "I can do *Muster Dogs*. I can get out, we can go regional,"' Monica says.

None of them realised just how tough it would be.

By the middle of 2020 they had two pregnant dogs, one on Joe Spicer's property in Hamilton, western Victoria, and another with Peter Barr in Pinnaroo, South Australia. Michael and the crew wanted to be able to film each birth, or at least be there as soon as possible afterwards. They didn't know which pups would end up being used in the series but getting the original footage was important. Cameraman Brad Smith (who happens to be married to *Muster Dogs* producer Monica) and sound recordist Jerry Batha drove 800 kilometres from Sydney to pick up Michael in Bendigo. They drove another 450 kilometres across the border to Pinnaroo and filmed Peter Barr's pregnant dog. They sensed the national mood around Covid was changing when their booking at the Pinnaroo motel was cancelled because they'd come from Victoria, where Covid numbers were skyrocketing; they were left to find a bed that night at short notice.

The next day they drove a few hours back across the border to Rob Tuncks's property in Edenhope to film the first big interview with him on his farm. While they were there the news came through that Peter Barr's pregnant dog was about to give birth. These could have been the *Muster Dogs* puppies and they needed those pictures. Michael, Brad and Jerry raced back to South Australia but were stopped by police at the border because they needed new permission letters. The police officer on border duty wasn't swayed by their pleas.

'We're here to do a TV series called *Muster Dogs*,' Michael told the cop. 'We're going straight to the property, we won't stop anywhere, we'll film them for exactly four hours and then we'll come straight back out here to you.'

The police officer looked at them and after a pause simply said no.

'Is that a big no? Or is it a maybe no?' Michael asked hopefully, as they pondered a Plan B.

It was a big no, and it was suddenly clear to all of them that filming this ambitious project during Covid was going to be a challenge.

'For that one moment when I was talking to the policeman on the border,' Michael said later, 'I thought, *I can just see*

Kelpie breeder Joe Spicer. (Steve Strike)

Frank Finger's champion dog, Annie, working the stock in *Muster Dogs* series one. (Steve Strike)

this all going to shit. After so many years of trying to make this show happen, it's about to go to shit.'

Just as they were about to give up, their phones pinged with the arrival of exemption emails. The police officer seemed just as relieved to be able to wave them through as they were to set off. They made it to Pinnaroo, but Peter's dog only delivered two puppies, not nearly enough for the show they had planned. They had five trainers lined up and they needed a dog each.

The filmmakers travelled back to Victoria and waited for the news from Joe Spicer. It came a couple of days later. The puppies had been born and there were plenty of them – black and red kelpies from the litter of parents, Truce and Bank, both multi-award-winning trial dogs with quality working dog bloodlines.

But there was still more drama to come. While they were filming the puppies, news came through that the border between Victoria and New South Wales was about to close. Hamilton is in the west of the state so Brad and Jerry quickly wrapped up the shoot and hit the road, with a six-hour drive ahead of them to avoid being trapped in Victoria.

By now it was July 2020 and most of Australia was hunkering down. The *Muster Dogs* team was trying to film a show that stretched from one coastline to another at a time when state and territory borders were shutting.

The puppies were to stay with Joe for three months before being sent to their new owners. Joe delivered Rob's puppy personally, while animal transporter Chet Simms was tasked with getting the other four puppies to their new owners: a 7000-kilometre puppy delivery service from Joe's place in western Victoria to Frank in central Queensland, up to CJ in the Northern Territory then over to Western Australia to Aticia and finally Joni (who named her puppy after him). Chet applied for special dispensation because he was moving stock.

Michael and Monica were always in the background thinking, *We've got our participants, we've got our puppies and we've got the best locations in the country, but can we get there, can we do this?*

The pandemic hovered over everything.

'It was like a flood coming down the river,' Michael told me. 'You can see it coming and you think, *I've got the sandbags there, but the walls are not high enough and, you know what, there is absolutely nothing I can do about it.*'

Michael, Brad and Jerry weren't the only members of the team scrambling to cross a border before it shut.

'We had filmed the birth of the puppies,' producer Monica told me. 'I was closing the finance on the series, and it was July 2020, and we knew New South Wales was going to go into lockdown in terms of the Queensland border. So Brad and I looked at each other and knew what we had to do.'

Brad and Monica packed up their kids and 12 cases of camera equipment overnight and drove north the next morning from their home in Sydney, arriving at the Queensland border four hours before it closed. With no *Muster Dogs* participants in New South Wales, it didn't make sense for them to be there.

'The only reason we were able to do that is because it wasn't going to cost the production any money because we could live with Brad's parents in Queensland,' Monica explained.

The family also spent weeks on end living in the Katherine Holiday Park in the Northern Territory. Monica was producing *Muster Dogs* and juggling another series she had underway, all while home-schooling the kids, who were aged six and ten.

Brad's job as director of photography – or DOP as they say in the trade – was to create 'the look' of the series. This means that no matter who's behind the camera you're getting a similar creative vision. It was particularly important on series one of *Muster Dogs*, when border closures, schedules and the number of participants meant that around 20 camera operators had input into the show.

The only state completely cut off from the film crew was Western Australia, so they hired freelancers in places like Broome, often ending up with camera operators whose experience was in regional TV advertisements, not documentary filmmaking.

Brad started out as a news cameraman for Channel 7 in Sydney and spent a lot of time working on reality TV shows, but documentaries were always 'the holy grail'. He brings a visual perspective that frames the whole series: from the 'newsy' moments that make you gasp, like the first sight of tiny new puppies, through to the beauty of following these determined people over this extraordinary terrain. Under Brad's guidance, the *Muster Dogs* series was like a treasure chest waiting to be opened.

'Shooting a show like this, to be honest, you don't have to try too hard,' he told me. 'You just have to get up early and shoot in good light. And besides, you're hanging out with real people, salt of the earth, and I think what farmers do is so critically important for the rest of us.'

In the past, camera crews on a shoot like this would have had to pay big bucks for helicopter flights to achieve the soaring panoramic shots they needed. These days there are drones in all the camera kits and Brad was able to get an aerial shot out of every crew. There was one moment from the first season that's stayed with him. He was filming CJ and Joe and their daughter, Lindsay, in the Northern Territory. They were mustering on horses and pushing the cattle up through the lush feed. Brad was using a combination of a handheld gimble, which stabilises the shot as you move the camera, a much larger long-lens camera, and a drone that he'd put into the sky above them.

'There were the ranges in front of them and dark thunderstorm clouds rolling in and then sunshine and a rainbow as well. I was multitasking with three cameras and trying to stay on task, but it was hard not to be gobsmacked.'

The show was filmed over the course of a year; borders opened, closed and opened again, often with just a few hours' notice; quarantine rules were relaxed and then reinforced; masks were on and off and back on again. Filming was coming to an end in June 2021, and after getting three shows in the can there was still the dramatic episode four, the climactic nail-biter finale, to go. For most of the participants, getting to the Northern Territory to film the finale wasn't the challenge it might have been even a year earlier. Aticia drove 1350 kilometres with Adam and Gossip to Perth and flew from there, while Joni drove across the border from Western Australia with Chet and some of her other dogs.

The final trial was held under near-perfect conditions, not far from CJ's home. Like so many of the shoots, not everything went to plan. I mean, they were working with animals, right? Cameraman Ben Emery turned up for the finale envisaging filming an 'epic cinematic landscape in the Top End at sunset', but things went quickly awry.

'The cattle got spooked by something,' he told me. 'I think it was [Rob's dog] Lucifer running into the middle of them – and they bolted, and within seconds they were just a dust storm on the horizon of these huge Northern Territory paddocks. CJ's husband had his dogs there on the sidelines and he just whistled at them and they leapt off the back of the motorbike. They'd been there the whole time, just focused and disciplined, and they took off out of sight and within five minutes they had the entire herd back. I'd never seen anything on that scale and it was just extraordinary to watch.'

Most of the participants in series one knew each other before signing up because of the working dog networks across the country. The producers had given them all strict instructions to avoid any contact in order to have maximum suspense when the cameras were rolling.

'Of course, being country people, we ignored the request, and all went boating on the river behind CJ's place with her husband, Joe, as tour guide,' Rob revealed later. 'Peter Barr saw a croc on the bank and wanted to touch it and the croc took one look at Pete and fled into the water. We were sneaking around trying to get a look at each other's dogs and then on the day we filmed we pretended we'd never seen each other.'

Rob had come north two months before the finale, leaving his wife and property in Victoria, because he was worried the border to the Northern Territory would close again. Rob had Lucifer with him through that long wait away from home, but he knew the mischievous companion wouldn't be coming home with him. They just weren't suited to each other and Lucifer wasn't up to the demands of sheep country. At that final moment of filming in episode four, when Rob told the other participants that he knew he couldn't keep his dog, no one was quite sure what would happen – and even Rob was wondering whether he'd auction Lucifer for charity. So it was a very special moment when Frank volunteered to take Lucifer off his hands.

'With these people, what you see is what you get,' Rob said, 'and, yes, Frank is genuinely that nice. When we were filming the final episode, my alternator failed and Frank had a spare battery that ran his car fridge. He sacrificed this and followed me to allow me to keep going by swapping my "flat" battery with his charged one every few hundred kilometres.'

*

With the filming all wrapped up, the editing hit top gear. It was only six months until air date. Everyone was feeling the pressure.

The ABC's Jo Chichester, who had first met with the team three years earlier, was feeling anxious. *Oh my God*, she kept thinking, *I'm going to lose my job*. Everything had been filmed beautifully and the characters were all there – but this type of format for television was new to all of them and she wasn't certain they had quite nailed it.

'We all believed in it, we all knew it was there and I just really wanted people to meet those characters and understand their lives,' she says. But the perfectionist in her kept worrying.

Experienced series editor John Unwin was feeling the pressure too. 'I'm not going to lie, it got pretty hectic and full-on towards the back end. In fact, I can say now it was the most challenging show I've ever worked on. But I don't often get to work on projects that mean so much to me.'

As a kid from a small town, John felt an affinity with *Muster Dogs*. He grew up in Woolgoolga, near Coffs Harbour, New South Wales. Back then it had a population of about 4000, and his family always had dogs.

'It wasn't until I moved away to the city that I didn't have a dog for the first time so it felt like such a big connection with the show,' he says. 'I just knew from the start it was bound to be, if not a success, at least loved.'

John spent hours in his dark edit suite in Brisbane. His 11-year-old golden retriever, Bailey, was a regular companion. While working on the edit, John built up a huge sound effects library of dog noises: puppies whinging, crying, scratching, shaking their collars. By the end, he could tell the pups apart by their barks.

'At the beginning of the edit Bailey would come running in with his ears perked up, thinking there was another dog in here with me, but after a month or so it was almost like he realised that it was all just bullshit. He was like, *No, that's not real. I'm not getting up for that trick anymore.*'

John crafted the show from hundreds of hours of footage, which had been filmed a variety of ways. A lot was shot by Brad and Ben, of course, but there was also the footage filmed by freelance camera operators in Western Australia who weren't used to shooting for documentaries. He had footage from drones and GoPros and even clips from the phones of the participants themselves.

He felt a connection to them all and lived through the rollercoaster of their lives – the death of Rob's dog Jumpy, Joni's fierceness but also her vulnerability in admitting she was lonely, Aticia's grim outlook about her drought-ridden property. He watched as CJ shed her initial cautiousness and as Frank grew into the role of mentor to them all. And he was there at the finale in the Northern Territory with all the participants and their dogs, something an editor doesn't normally get to do. It only heightened his determination to make sure the participants were happy. 'They were worried they'd be made to look stupid,' he says. 'It took a lot to get their trust and keep it.'

John had worked on plenty of other reality TV shows, but this was the first time his father was proud to tell his mates what his son was doing.

*

So, despite the challenges, there were no regrets. It was exactly as they had all hoped – an inspiring and beautiful four hours of television. But what was it that made *Muster Dogs* such a success?

Jo Chichester reckons that audiences enjoyed its gentleness, at a time when their own daily lives had been so bruising. She knows that successful television can often be about timing. *Muster Dogs* had authentic characters and the irresistible lure of puppies. But the producers weren't to know it would hit screens just as the pandemic was easing, following a period when dog ownership had increased across the country and house-locked Australians had sought the company and warmth of a new pet.

'Marc Fennell, who produced a show called *Stuff the British Stole*, says that a really good idea in factual TV production is [exploring] something that people think they know about, but you're showing them something they don't know,' she says.

People were fascinated with the training process but also enjoyed learning about the role dogs played on farms, carrying out work that might have otherwise been done by machines and farmhands.

More than a million people watched on that first night back in 2022. And millions more have watched since then. No one would have predicted that a show about a bundle of puppies being trained in the stark outback of Australia could take the nation by storm.

But one thing was certain, people couldn't get enough of it, and so it was only natural that the ABC signed up for season two. Time to do it all again.

CHAPTER 2

Select, Breed, Hope

Let me share a little secret. I was the last addition to the *Muster Dogs* team, and I almost didn't become a part of it at all.

The concept of the *Muster Dogs* series hadn't been tackled before so the creative team was making it as they went along. In the TV world, that means there are things that will happen naturally, and other things – the technical bits like the edit and graphics and music – that require a lot of brain power.

All of those elements determine the tone of the show. The producers knew they wanted a female narrator and it was important to the creative team that the 'voice' had an authenticity to viewers in regional Australia. They'd been tossing around a few options without pinpointing names. They wanted a voice that had a timbre that wouldn't be jarring when edited in with the participants', a voice that would sit in balance with theirs, with an empathy and connection to the country.

Well, that's what they told me. I suspect there were a few names ahead of mine, but I will be eternally grateful for the phone call that came on a Friday afternoon in October 2021 from Jo Chichester, who told me about a little show they'd like me to narrate, in part because I grew up in the country.

I'll never tire of saying those words – I grew up in the country – despite living a life that each year has taken me further from where it all started.

Before I was born, Mum and Dad had followed their dreams and become dairy farmers, first in Biloela in central Queensland and then in Kilkivan in the South Burnett area. But after 20 years of milking, Dad developed a skin condition, and the Jersey cows, whose faces Mum thought were filled with kindness, had to go. By the time I was born, they'd sold all but half a dozen cows and some pigs. There was no question of leaving Kilkivan at that time, though. They still had access to the land outside of town near the showgrounds, so Dad turned his attention to crops and growing grain and lucerne and baling hay to bring in money. Years later an ABC viewer sent me a letter. She'd been clearing out her mother's house after her mother's death and found a receipt that Dad had written, his neat handwriting indicating he'd sold her some hay worth $1 a bale in 1968.

Mum and Dad had three children – Robert, David and Wendy – but only Wendy was still living at home when they decided to 'go again'. Robert was already earning money as a young teller at a bank in Gympie. David was doing his final years of high school at boarding school because classes at the local school stopped after Grade Ten; for kids in Kilkivan, it was either boarding school or a long bus trip every day further west to Murgon.

Wendy was in Grade Nine and just about to turn 14 when I was born. None of the family can remember much about my birth or whether Mum endured a long labour, almost an hour's drive from the nearest medical care. David, who was 16, remembers Dad had a Ford Fairlane Compact V8, a nugget of detail offered up half a century later that reveals exactly where my brother's priorities lay at the time.

A couple of years later, another baby came along: a gorgeous fair-haired, chubby-cheeked girl named Trudi. We discovered when we were older that the women in town, who'd planned a welcome-home morning tea for Mum and the new baby, greeted her with 'Ah, so here is Lisa's playmate.' And she was indeed a great playmate; we spent most of our time outside in the house yard, digging channels through Mum's rose garden and taking valuable water from the tank to create riverways for our toy ships.

One day when I was still just a toddler, my brother David spotted me bolting down the road into town. Always the joker, David reckons he and Mum disagreed on the best action to take. Thankfully, she won and went after me. I never really stopped travelling.

It feels like I've been on the move for 50 years now – from Kilkivan to the nearest big town of Gympie when I was ten and then to Brisbane for university and the start of a career that led me overseas. I was still only 16 during Orientation Week at Queensland University and I remember feeling completely out of my depth, younger than the others because of where I grew up. There were no preschool options in Kilkivan, or day care or kindergarten, and the minute you were old enough to start Grade One you had a school uniform on and were packed off with 10 cents for a Chiko Roll at lunchtime. I can still remember the terror of turning up to my first day of school being separated properly for the first time from Mum.

I had no complaints, though. That country upbringing didn't stop me following my dreams and becoming a foreign correspondent for more than a decade, reporting in 40 different countries through some turbulent years.

No matter how far I went, I never lost that feeling of connection with rural Australia. When Jo called on that Friday afternoon to ask if I would narrate a TV series about dogs, I was thrilled. There was a caveat – they were just sounding me out and it wasn't locked in that I'd get the gig. She asked me

Here I am as a toddler, mustering at Kilkivan, Queensland. Only later did I learn it is easier when working dogs were involved.

to record some audio of myself on my phone to send to the producers as an audition. They knew what my voice sounded like as a news presenter, but could I cut it as a narrator for a feature show? After a couple of attempts they decided to give me a shot.

I've done a lot of things during my 30-plus years as a journalist. I've reported on some of the biggest stories in the world. I had a front-row seat in the US as it wrestled with the war on terror, I watched Beijing host what would be the last extravagant Olympics of our era, and stood outside the chapel in Windsor as Harry and Meghan exchanged vows. But recording that first session of narration for *Muster Dogs* was a completely different sort of challenge and one that I thought might be beyond me.

I'd been up since 3am and had co-hosted three hours of live television that morning. The TV studios and newsroom in Melbourne are on the ground floor but I was going to be recording in one of the audio studios upstairs, large enough to fit a sound desk and a few people – not that there was anyone in there with me. Covid lockdowns meant I connected via my laptop with ABC producer Rachel Robinson in Sydney as well as with Monica, who sat propped on her parents-in-law's bed in Brisbane, where she remained trapped by border closures. We made slow headway, sentence by sentence, over several hours.

The instructions came thick and fast. Just be conversational and try to have a little smile in your voice at that point halfway through the sentence. Can you give us several options there please, ending with an upward and downward inflection? Now you're coming off the vision of the puppy tilting its head, so can you sound quizzical?

I knew how much was at stake and I was desperate to deliver, but I felt like I was auditioning for a spot at drama school. And it didn't help that I'd been up, and talking, since 3am. I stumbled home and rang my best friend, almost in tears by this point. Leigh Sales and I have shared career highs and lows and sought advice from each other since we met at a work dinner almost 30 years ago. It was an ABC farewell, or birthday, or celebration, or commiseration; we can't remember the occasion, but we were the first ones there and we confessed to each other that we couldn't be late even when we tried and – sigh – if only the rest of the world was as punctual. We've been friends ever since.

'I've bitten off more than I can chew. It's too hard, I can't do it,' I told her, slumped on the couch at home in Melbourne.

'Can you pull out?' she asked, surprising me with her response. She was normally the first to encourage me to 'drink a cup of concrete and harden up'. But she could tell from the tiredness in my voice that I felt beaten by it. It's taken years of hosting breakfast television to appreciate the accumulative effect of sleep deprivation.

It's also remarkable how things look different in the bright light of a new day and thankfully we agreed I should push on.

My involvement with series two couldn't have been more different. It seemed an unspoken given that I'd be part of the team again, and I was introduced much earlier to the filming plans. I met most of the participants while production was still underway and spent time with them at their homes and with their families, assuring them that their nerves and hesitations had been shared by everyone in season one as well.

But this season *was* different. The second group of participants *knew* they were signing up to a hit show and with that came a different kind of pressure. And there was pressure for the producers as well.

So how do you take an unexpected success story and try to do it all over again? That was the herculean task facing the *Muster Dogs* team. They mulled over ideas for months and then they decided to try to repeat the winning formula by changing the dog breed from kelpies to border collies. Their first job was to breed some pups.

*

Shortly after 4pm on a cold winter afternoon on a farm near Dubbo in New South Wales, Debbie started giving birth.

This was no ordinary birthing process. The border collie's litter would be the next stars of *Muster Dogs*. Debbie had been pregnant for nine weeks, an average time for dogs, but her belly was so swollen that her owner, Carolyn Hudson, knew this would not be an average litter. They'd had the vet do an ultrasound but there were so many pups wriggling around overlapping each other inside Debbie that they couldn't be certain where one began and another one finished. All they knew was that it could be easily more than half a dozen.

It was 21 June 2022 and Carolyn had brought Debbie inside two days earlier, into the warmth of her big country kitchen. The expectant mum had started to go off her food, one of the first signs of an impending birth. A slow-combustion stove burned in the corner and Carolyn kept Debbie in a timber whelping box on the other side of the room to make sure she didn't overheat. Everything had to be just right.

Carolyn watched as Debbie started scratching at the sheet that had been laid down for her. If Debbie had been outside, she would have been digging her hole in the dirt, instinctively making a confined space to keep her babies safe and predatory dingoes at bay. Carolyn knew that the birth couldn't be far away. Debbie was increasingly restless and had stopped eating anything but little bits of minced meat. Then the contractions began – big deep breaths from Debbie who was now lying on her side, her body tensing up as she prepared to birth the first pup.

Carolyn had watched over the births of dozens of puppies over the years and almost all of them had arrived late in the day, sometimes deep into the night. She sometimes wondered if night-time births were also part of a protection mechanism for mums. But not for Debbie, whose puppies started arriving while the sun was still out.

At 4.15pm the first puppy emerged. Carolyn sat quietly by, making sure Debbie could break the protective foetal membrane and help the pup squirm its way to her teat. Puppies don't open their eyes for at least two weeks so everything at this point is on their mum and her human helpers.

The speed of the first arrival caught the film crew off guard; they were filming elsewhere on the farm and missed it. But they quickly returned and waited. And waited. They started to worry that maybe their presence was putting Debbie off. But finally another pup arrived, and then a couple more. It was a slow process and there were a lot of pups – each birth sapping Debbie's strength. Carolyn and her husband, Mick, took shifts, topping bits of sausage with calcium powder or liquid to feed to Debbie to replace the essential minerals she was losing each time she pushed a pup out. They changed the sheeting occasionally but otherwise tried not to intervene and let nature take its course.

'Come on, old girl,' they encouraged her, knowing her instincts would kick in each time.

Close to midnight, Carolyn told Mick he was on solo duties while she took a 30-minute nap. She was exhausted.

While Carolyn was asleep, Debbie birthed another two pups. Mick had to gently pull one of them out and break the fluid-filled sac in which it was born. But Debbie still wasn't finished.

'By the end I also had to help another one out and break the sac, she was just so, so tired,' Carolyn recalls. Carolyn rubbed her hand along Debbie's side, feeling for any hardness that would indicate there were more pups still to come. It was a long night for everyone but 14 hours later they were all done. They had ten healthy pups ready to be the stars of the second *Muster Dogs* series and Debbie was ready to sleep.

Mick and Carolyn's dogs have pedigrees going back a hundred years, and Mick has two generations of reputation behind him. His dad and grandfather were also breeders and renowned dog educators. His dad, Pip, won major titles as a trialler, including the Supreme Australian Championship for working sheep dogs. Pip's father won the Champion of Champions in the 1950s. And Mick started competing in dog trial championships when he was 16.

'There's an old saying,' Mick says. 'Select the best, breed from the best and hope for the best.' The Hudsons know how to select dogs for natural ability, stamina, trainability, size and strength. It's a long list and it's fascinating to see what can be accentuated or diminished as you decide which dogs to mate. We'll go into that in detail later but for now Mick and Carolyn's job had been done, producing the best litter possible for a new batch of *Muster Dogs* graziers and trainers across Australia.

*

Despite growing up in rural Australia I don't know that I ever saw puppies being born. Almost everyone had a dog or two of some sort, but a lot of them had been desexed. You didn't just breed a dog because you could, otherwise you'd end up passing on weaknesses like biting.

My younger sister, Trudi, and I had a dog called Mack, a black and white border collie cross with the gentlest of natures and softest of hair. We don't remember where he came from, but he was a constant throughout our childhood and, if truth be told, he had a pretty cushy life in Kilkivan. Trudi always had a natural affinity with animals, in particular the four-legged kind. She'd be on the ground cuddling them while I kept my distance until I could be sure about their intentions. Despite Mack's nature I still found him a little intimidating as he wielded his authority around the yard. There were no animals to muster but his attempts to show the chickens who was boss left them less than impressed.

Mack was what you might call a house dog, although that description is a bit of a misnomer. I grew up believing the world was split into people who let their dogs come inside (otherwise known as city people) and the rest of us who thought a dog's place was absolutely, most definitely, outside. If a dog on a farm was described as a 'house dog', it was probably because they occupied the veranda, and only if they were very lucky. Never was that more apparent to me than when Mum and Dad sold our home in Kilkivan, and the new owners arrived with a scruffy little thing that immediately ran through the house and claimed ownership. I thought my mother would faint.

Despite almost four decades passing since my family left Kilkivan, we've never lost our connection with the town. In fact, in 2023 I went back to give a talk at the local bowls club to help raise funds for the kindergarten. My Grade One teacher, Miss Bishop, was in the audience that day, and so was Mrs Farrow, who used to run the post office and the telephone switchboard. My sister Trudi came with me and we reminisced the whole way.

There was another reason that made that trip to Kilkivan special. I'd been let in on the secret location of one of the next *Muster Dogs* participants, just up the road in Ban Ban Springs.

The pups that Mick and Carolyn had helped see into the world had spent a few months with them in Dubbo before heading off to their new homes. And the five new participants couldn't wait to meet them.

Everyone has their own story of how they became part of this show. Certainly, after the success of the first series, there was a flood of applications from people wanting to join the next series. I received personal pleas from viewers hoping that I had some sway with the producers (I did not).

The actual process of finding the participants was long and involved a lot of brainstorming among the team. At the core of the producers' decisions was a need to get the greatest variety of people, experiences and landscapes. For some of the hopefuls, it was the urging of their young children that made them apply. Some had been encouraged by experts in the industry after they'd witnessed them at dog schools. Some were simply word of mouth. There was not one single secret to the process, but the producers knew what they wanted – the magic ingredients for another brilliant show.

Once the five participants had been selected and given their dogs, the film crew turned up every few months to see how they were progressing. I followed most of their progress from home in Melbourne, hearing tales of triumph and heartache from the producers.

Finally, though, as I started working on my own project – this book – I was able to hit the road and meet them myself. And Cilla, in Ban Ban Springs, would be the first. My sister Trudi drove us out of Kilkivan towards the Burnett Highway – a name that suggests a much grander road than the reality, with great stretches of it still narrowing to a single lane.

'Don't go off the road, you doofus!' she vented at an oncoming car.

It was one of the first rules we learned as kids about driving in the country. If someone coming towards you had already moved off the road onto the gravel shoulder, you should stay on the bitumen. No point both of you getting off and ending up in trouble. Windscreens didn't so much crack in those days as shatter into tiny blue-green shards if a small stone hit its mark. I remember picking out pieces of glass from under the floormat as we made a slow journey home after one such occasion.

Rule number two was always 'give the country wave', a casual lift of the fingers from the steering wheel at whoever was whizzing past.

Muster Dogs participant Cilla Pershouse had given us the kind of instructions you get in the country, where isolation puts distances into perspective – drive 80 kilometres, then a couple more kilometres after the turn, then look for a driveway a few kilometres long.

As we pulled up at her house, a little Maltese shih-tzu bounded out to give us a once over, before Cilla appeared with a baby boy propped on her hip. She called out to the tiny four-legged guard-dog, Minty, to let us into the yard. Her long blonde hair was tied in a twisted bun that popped through a hole she'd made in the top of her big straw hat. She offered us tea and we stood in the kitchen talking for so long we forgot the jug had boiled and already started cooling.

'What's with the shih-tzu?' I asked, curious to find a designer dog on a property a long way from anywhere.

'Oh, I inherited Minty from some people who were allergic to her furry coat, but she's a little Houdini and is *supposed* to stay on the veranda,' she told us. 'She was great when she used to come on the road with me when we were performing the kids' concerts.'

Cilla has crammed a lot into her 38 years. She was born close to where she now lives and was home-educated by parents who wanted their four children to find their individual strengths and follow their dreams. One of Cilla's brothers founded a small mill at the age of 17 and within a few decades was overseeing one of the biggest privately owned sawmills in southeast Queensland. Her other brother went straight into farming and her sister became a potter and painter. Cilla wanted to be a dancer.

'There was no musical background in the family, but I was always a dancer and went to dance classes, and Mum would take me to competitions and be travelling further and further because there was nothing around here.'

Eventually she left to study musical theatre in Mackay before working in Brisbane and then Sydney. She became a city chick. 'I went from being a big fish in a little pond to being a teeny-tiny little plankton in the ocean.'

She worked harder and pedalled faster but could never get ahead. She was nearly 30 and questioning what it was all about when she went home to country Queensland for Christmas one year and realised she'd hit the wall. She returned just once more to Sydney and that was to pack up her life and her car and drive the 14 hours north, back to her family.

'I never thought I'd move back to the bush. I thought I was a different person. But it actually turns out: what I *was* was a performer, but who I *am* is a country person.'

We were sitting quietly on the veranda as she reached for the words. My sister Trudi, who has three grown-up children of her own and often wonders what it would be like to move back to the country, had taken the baby for a walk to give Cilla the space to talk about that decision to step off centre stage. Cilla is the one in the marriage who runs the property and dreams of being a 'big-time cattle farmer', while her husband, Scott, works for her family's timber company.

'I feel very at home here. It's a beautiful place, beautiful on all levels – beautiful to look at, but it's very productive,' she said. 'The cattle do well here, and the garden is incredible. We'd love to buy more land, but we can't afford it. So we've just got to keep saving up and hope that we can grow our holdings here.'

We were still talking when Scott arrived home with four-year-old Greta and two-year-old Annie. The children were newly at kindergarten in Biggenden, about half an hour away. 'We've just started navigating this new stage of "Holy shit, I have to drive two hours a day to get my kids to kindergarten and back,"' Cilla said. But she wanted to make sure they played with other children, and separating the young sisters seemed almost cruel. Greta did one day at kindy by herself, and Annie wandered around lost, wondering where her playmate had gone.

Kindergarten had added another complication for Cilla to a daily routine that was simple, albeit sometimes challenging. 'I need to be pretty self-sufficient because Scott works off-farm, so the kids and I just head off – we pack the dogs in, and we check the cattle, especially during weaning, and do the circuit. We're a good little team, but we trundle most of the time. This whole property is their backyard.'

And the dogs are constant companions. There are three mature border collies – Molly, Maggie and Frankie – and two young ones. 'Maggie is our strongest working dog – she's incredible, a tiny little thing who's got so much passion, a real leader. Frankie is a goofball and we've got Foxy who's in training.' And they also have Axel, a pure-bred kelpie, 'who is going to be the next superstar'.

Minty, who we met when we arrived, is a cheeky bugger, according to Cilla. She sometimes sneaks into the ute and ends up on a mustering adventure.

'When I send the dogs, if I give the command, Minty will take off up the paddock and she looks like a little bunny rabbit. *Ding, ding, ding, ding* – off around the cows she goes and she thinks, *This is my job, I'm off with the dogs*, but I'm worried she'll get lost or eaten by an eagle, she's so small. But she loves it. Molly is my favourite dog and she's getting older too, and that brings up a whole other thing of ... Well, they don't live long enough and she's going to have to retire from working soon, so she's big shoes to fill.'

Before Cilla met Scott, and way before children came along, she'd had another creation in mind: a children's music and dance show, to make sure kids in the bush could have the same opportunities as city kids. She'd toyed with the idea when she'd been living in Sydney, and once back with her family she brought it to life, eventually taking it on the road. She met Scott at the timber mill where she was working, and he happily signed up to be a roadie for the dozen or so shows they did each year. When Greta was born, they took her too. Things slowed down a little after the arrival of Annie and baby Sidney, but Cilla has never lost that desire to try to bridge the gap between city and country.

Muster Dogs appeared in her life at just the right time. This effervescent, impatient creative artist had been feeling flat and overwhelmed, and if she'd been closer to a doctor or had time to look after herself, she might well have been diagnosed with postnatal depression.

'I never truly understood mental health struggles until I had Sidney and I was like, "Ohhh, I get it, I understand," and I was frightened that I couldn't snap out of that feeling.'

It seems counterintuitive that at her lowest moment, when she felt exhausted and lost, she would sign up to a national television program, but that's what she did.

'My mum had a bad accident working cattle and while she was laid up she discovered *Muster Dogs* and kept telling me how wonderful it was. And then along came the call-out for people wanting to take on a border collie.'

Cilla has always thought of her relationship with working dogs as being like a rehearsal and performance. What you do in rehearsal will determine how good your performance will be.

'You can't *not* rehearse and then just be an absolute showstopper. The foundations are your rehearsal and that's your training. That's you working together.'

Cilla named her new *Muster Dogs* puppy Ash Barky, in honour of Australia's queen of the tennis court Ash Barty, and it didn't take long for the pup to draw her out of her funk. As she showed us the dance tricks she'd been practising with Ash on the lawn, the kids joined in. It had been like that since the little border collie joined the family. 'I'm running around like a bloody idiot and the kids are loving it and it's something we're all doing together. I need to be on my game for that little doggo,' she told me.

She did wonder if she'd chosen the right name for her. 'The kids can't say Ash and they call her Ass,' she admitted with a laugh. 'All I can hear is them saying, "Come on, Ass, come here, little Ass."'

It gets worse. Cilla's dog Axel has proved to be a difficult name for the children to say as well. 'I swear it sounds like they're saying, "Asshole, good dog, Asshole" – so it's Ass and Asshole.' She dissolved into giggles at the thought of it.

*

Back home in Melbourne I checked the map of Australia and started plotting another trip. Some of the participants were going to prove just too hard to get to – their locations so remote. But with some spare time from my day job on breakfast TV, I reckoned I could get down to Tasmania to meet Russ Fowler and his family on their farm.

Part of the *Muster Dogs* appeal for viewers is the surprise factor and that's meant participants have had to keep their own involvement as closely guarded as they can. So what happens when you live in a small town on an island and everyone knows your business?

Charlie was always going to be the worst keeper of secrets. When his dad, Russ, signed up to become a participant in series two, Charlie was told under no circumstances, not any, was he allowed to tell anyone. But try explaining that to a four-year-old.

'We went to the Bream Creek dog show just yesterday,' Russ told me when I met him, 'and I said, "Now, Charlie, we can't mention our Muster Dog," and then I saw Frank Finger who'd been invited as a special guest and I got so excited I thought it's actually *me* that's going to have trouble staying quiet.'

Charlie had been besotted by the first series, so when Russ spotted the social media post seeking interest from anyone wanting to sign up for the new season, he jumped at the chance. He sent a three-minute video as part of the audition, filmed on a hilltop on his farm near Bothwell in central Tasmania; it was a picturesque scene with the young farmer and his sheep, his dogs holding them in place.

Russ comes from a long line of farmers, and he's never been without dogs, mostly huntaways from New Zealand, a few kelpies and some border collies. He hadn't felt nervous when he'd heard the news that he'd be part of the show but, by the time the new puppy arrived, the Fowler family was juggling a lot. A new baby – a little sister for Charlie who

Cilla Pershouse was the first participant I met in series two. She lives 'up the road' from where I grew up in Kilkivan. (Trudi Melloy)

Russ Fowler's son, Charlie, loved Molly from the start. (Brad Smith)

they named Milly – had been born just weeks earlier. And the puppy from Mick Hudson's litter was clearly a larrikin who was best described as goofy. They named her Molly. Milly and Molly – no surprises they've confused the two.

'But my wife did it before me, so I was let off the hook,' Russ said, laughing.

He'd met Rosie in Western Australia while jackarooing, a requirement of the agribusiness management course he studied in Geelong. Her family owned the farm next door.

'The fences weren't good enough on the boundary so I snuck across,' he told me with a chuckle.

Russ had seemed destined to be a farmer. He'd come home from primary school on the bus during shearing season, busting to get amongst it, penning up the sheep ready for the workers. He went away to boarding school when he was older but was home every weekend to work on the family farm. But when the time came to make the decision to follow in his father's footsteps, it wasn't automatic. He headed to South Africa and spent 12 months getting a different perspective on life, to see if something was missing. His biggest fear was committing to the family business back in Tasmania and then, after five years, deciding he wanted out.

He'd learned from watching his dad run the farm that change can be forced on you – whether in response to technology or the increasingly uncertain environment. Russ respected how his father had been at the forefront of innovation for his generation, but he knew he'd have to make his own changes to keep the property financially and environmentally sustainable. And sometimes change happens when you least expect it – and it can leave you reeling.

In early October 2019, Rosie returned from visiting family in Western Australia and noticed a persistent bruise on her thigh. She'd fallen off a chair but hadn't thought much of it until she was back home in the small town of Bothwell and noticed how big the bruise was. She was tired and lethargic but put that down to caring for a nine-month-old. The bruise, though, was something else. She'd been home for a couple of days when she popped into the local doctor's surgery.

They did some blood tests and she anticipated hearing nothing more than confirmation she was a tired young mum. The phone call came at 10pm, never a good time to be hearing from a doctor.

'He wanted her to go straight down to the hospital in Hobart, about an hour away, in the morning,' Russ told me. 'He didn't really divulge too much but it could have been a couple of things and leukaemia was one of them.'

Rosie was admitted at the Royal Hobart Hospital by 7am and within hours they had the diagnosis: blood cancer, acute myeloid leukaemia. It was devastating for all of them, this young family with an almost-toddler and a farm to run.

'I was effectively emotionally numb, I didn't know how I felt because it all happened so quickly,' Russ said, recounting those early days. 'I tried to be her rock, not be a worrier and just deal with what I could.'

It was a blur – the abrupt end to breastfeeding for Charlie, the urgent need for accommodation near the hospital, the daily trek for Russ and little Charlie to see Rosie in the ward, wondering if the chemotherapy was taking effect. Rosie's mum, Alison, a schoolteacher in Western Australia, dropped everything to be with them and Russ had no choice but to leave the farm in the hands of his staff. That was no small feat. They had four farms, with thousands of cattle and sheep. Russ was the seventh generation to care for the property and he'd always approached his duties with a determination to leave the land in better condition than when he arrived. He didn't see the farm as his; he considered himself a caretaker for the next generation. But he couldn't give it the attention it needed. He'd try to get back for a day once a week and he'd always find his dogs waiting for his vehicle, eager to work for him. In their own way they were trying to make his life easier.

'Their loyalty, their commitment, they can read you like a book,' he said.

When the family emerged from the fog, and with Rosie in remission, they started putting their life back together. Rosie returned to her trade of hairdressing; two years later another baby arrived, and then Russ signed up for *Muster Dogs*. Maybe it was Charlie's obsession with the kelpies from series one, maybe it was Rosie's brush with death and the feeling that they should take opportunities when they came. But there was no doubt Russ was a farmer with an eye on the future. He wanted to be part of the change, not wait for it to happen to him.

'I see my job as no different to that of a CEO of a big business where financial and environmental decisions have to be made,' he said. 'I mean, it's not to say Rosie's sickness and everything that went on is totally in the rear-view mirror but it's really nice that we can move on with the next chapter.'

*

Our next participant was not so easy to get to. And even harder to get on the phone. Wilcannia is a small town in northwestern New South Wales with a population of around 700. It's home to Lily Davies-Etheridge – that is, when she's there. The busy contract musterer is often on the road but we eventually caught up on the phone and I asked her how hard it was as a kid having to leave the property to return to boarding school.

It was never the best day, she said, that last sunrise of the holidays when she knew she had to go back to school. It wasn't that she didn't like it there; she just liked being on her family's property so much more. Her mum, Mog, would make promises they both knew were simply wishful thinking – that before she knew it another term would be over and she'd be back swimming in the billabongs, riding the horses and playing with her dogs again. As the bus took her closer to the regional centre of Orange and she'd get her first glimpse of the grand red-brick school buildings, she would start wishing the hours away.

'I'd be cooped up in a boarding house and sitting at a desk when all I wanted to do was be outside, doing something more productive than sitting down all day,' Lily said.

Until she went to high school, Lily hadn't known anything other than Kalyanka Station, a 50,000-hectare sheep and goat property that stretches down to the banks of the Darling–Baaka River. Her parents bought it a decade before she was born and Lily grew up there with her sister, Clancy.

'I loved being home-schooled through School of the Air in the early years because you'd get a week's worth of school work done in a few days and then you could go and play with the dog or hop on your horse and you could help with the property,' she said.

Mog reckoned it wasn't just the dogs; it was the chickens that captivated Lily first. 'By the time she was eight she was always walking around with a chook under her arm or on her shoulder and she'd enter them in the country show,' Mog said. 'She used to write down all their pedigrees and which chickens and hens were what; she's like that now with horses and dogs.'

The property is just down the road from the small town of Wilcannia. 'A pub and a shop and a golf course' is how

Lily describes it. It costs you four dollars to play the nine-hole sand course, half that if you're a member. After 6pm they'll only serve you light beer, and closing hours depend on 'patron behaviour'. The slogan for the Wilcannia Tourism Association is 'Middle of Nowhere, Centre of Everywhere', and while the town used to be a thriving river port back in the nineteenth century with paddle-steamers plying the riverway, its heritage sandstone facades now belie the town's diminishing fortunes. It's an 11-hour drive to get to the state's capital, but Sydney may as well be on another planet. Mog, with a talent for painting, studied there for a while at the renowned National Art School in Darlinghurst. But in the end the pull of the land brings them all home.

It can be an unforgiving part of Australia. I spent time there filming a story for *Back Roads* for the ABC when the floodplains were dry and the nearby Menindee Lakes, which are supposed to be the water supply for the region, had been long drained. Fish were dying in areas that should have been brimming with wildlife, and local Barkindji people spoke to me of the dismay they felt about the treatment of their land. The politics of water, who gets it and when, hangs over this region.

But this is home for Lily Davies-Etheridge, a unique place she says, and she wouldn't want to be anywhere else. She had the chance to leave. Her marks were so good at school she could have studied veterinary science and she might still. But she delayed her acceptance and was going to take a gap year, and then Covid happened and then, well, it just seemed like Kalyanka was her happy place.

She takes contract work to muster on properties in the area. Sometimes the jobs are just a day here and there, but she prefers the longer stints when she packs up her kit and loads her two kelpies, Raffy and Candy, into the ute and off she goes, sometimes hundreds of kilometres. She'll sometimes listen to music or call friends to pass the time. If she has service.

'It's better for me to not be spending hours on the road getting somewhere for just a day's work so I try to take the bigger jobs and it can be anything, goats, cattle, sheep,' she told me. A lot of it has been rounding up feral goats, especially around Cobar, and that can be hard work. You need big teams for that, including bikes and helicopters, because it's big and wild country.

Landowners pay Lily, with her dogs and motorbike, to bring in the feral goats, which are then sold for their meat.

'The goats are an easy way for people to make money – you haven't spent anything on them because they're wild. They're popular, I don't know why, they're pretty rough and stinky.'

But just when she was getting plenty of work for goats, the prices 'went to shit', as she describes it. The sheep price is more constant and remains a cornerstone of what she does.

She comes as a package, Lily and her dogs, and the regulars are always checking to see if she can take a job, partly because there just aren't enough people who want to do the work she does. And besides, others will say, she's very good.

'The only certainty is that the day always starts early but I could be out bush or doing yard work, whatever they need, and if it's a big job you'll definitely have air support,' she explained over the crackly phone line.

She's never lonely, catching up with friends on different jobs or at gymkhanas and rodeos or the races. Even going into town to stock up on things is a chance to be social. From a distance it could seem like an unusual life for this easy-going blonde 21-year-old, heading off in the ute by herself, sharing quarters with the bushmen of Australia, always on the move. She's not bothered by the ribald humour. In fact, she's the first to admit she'll have a laugh with the others and join in. 'It's not coming from a bad place, no one is saying it to be a creep, there's no threat.'

But one thing is sure to trigger a fiery reaction. 'It annoys me when someone presumes I can't do something because I'm female.' She knows what she's doing when she's out there working her dogs and it's part of the reason she decided to take part in this second series. 'I was debating whether to go to uni or not, but I wanted to find a reason to keep doing what I love doing.'

She is part of a new generation of farmer. Her mum has passed on the determination to leave the land in better shape than when they got there, teaching her daughter about regenerative agriculture and grazing and repairing the damage done by old-style land use.

Lily knows how much dogs are a part of that. 'Educated dogs,' she said, quickly correcting herself.

When the little white puppy with one black ear arrived from Mick and Carolyn Hudson's litter, the fact it was a male was a surprise. Apart from her sister's boyfriend, it had been just her and Clancy and Mog for a while.

'And I've always worked with kelpies so it's different for me having a border collie, but he's quickly become my main man,' she said of Snow, her *Muster Dogs* pup.

Lily won't describe herself this way but she's so talented with her stock and the dogs that she seems old beyond her 21 years. She is determined, stubborn and tough on herself. 'I'm never quite satisfied. I'll analyse why things might have gone wrong with training, whether it's the horses or the dogs. But I don't know if I'm a perfectionist; if you look at my ute, it's an absolute pigsty so it just depends!'

*

Let's head 1500 kilometres north from Wilcannia to Winton to meet another of our series two participants.

The bar at the North Gregory Hotel in outback Queensland was full of grey nomads, who'd arrived that day in their attempt to flee the cold winter months down south. It was

Lily Davies-Etheridge's pup Snow. (Sally Browning)

Keri Prandolini's dog Bobby McGee (left) trained alongside Steve Elliott's dog Indi. (Melissa Spencer)

just after dinner when a young fellow called Harry challenged Steve, our *Muster Dogs* participant, to a game of pool. I asked Harry how he was going to approach the opening break as he set up the triangle and steadied the balls.

'I like to smash it first and see where they go,' he said, with all the authority of a professional player as he swaggered over to take one last sip of his drink.

Steve inspected his cue and watched as Harry set the game in motion with an almighty bang. No balls in. Harry's technique hadn't worked and he shook his head in frustration.

Steve prowled the table and then proceeded to pot one ball after another. Finally, he faltered and Harry got his chance. He managed to sink a couple before a missed shot left Steve to plant the black and claim victory.

'You guys have clearly played before,' I said, quietly dropping my early ambitious thought of challenging the winner.

'A few times,' Steve said with a laugh as he pushed the electronic lever on his wheelchair to head to the bar. And no doubt there'll be a few times more. Harry's hoping that once he turns ten and has grown a bit more, he might have more of a chance against his older friend.

There's not much Steve Elliott can't do. And don't bother asking him about the accident that put him in the chair, paralysed from the chest down, because he's not interested in something that happened a couple of decades ago. I've gleaned a little from news reports from the time. He was in his late twenties, working a night job baking bread in his parents' bakery in Winton, doing a bit of cattle mustering on the side during the day and following his passion of bareback riding at rodeos. On New Year's Eve 2003 he was competing at the Black River rodeo near Townsville when his foot got caught as he came off a bucking bronc. He returned home to Winton seven months later in a wheelchair.

'Most people call it a disability, I just call it a wheelchair,' he said when I asked him about that time. He's got about half a dozen battery-powered wheelchairs, their solid tyres thick with the dust of a dry country town. One of them is a modified Segway with two wheels, which he manoeuvres with ease. I did a Segway tour once of Washington DC when my niece and her husband were visiting me there and we all nearly came off at one point or another. Steve tells me he's been bucked off once or twice and he needs a hand to get back on. He's determinedly independent, often obstinately so, according to his friend Keri Prandolini, who drives 700 kilometres from her home northwest of Cairns every second week to give him a hand. When I visited, she had an electric fence to put up and a bit of gardening to do. And she's had to become a ready wheelchair mechanic.

It was Keri who'd initially applied for a shot at *Muster Dogs*, delivering a compelling video audition. But there were hundreds of applications and the producers were looking to find the right mix of landscapes and locations, genders and experience levels. They approached Steve, whose name kept coming up among dog enthusiasts, without realising that Keri was his great mate. Getting Steve involved meant viewers got to see Keri in action as well and it set the stage for some friendly competition.

Their relationship has all the barbs and zings of a long and comfortable friendship. They met a couple of years after Steve's accident, when Keri's eldest son, now 18, was just a toddler. 'I've always called him "Hollywood" because somebody wants to take a photo or they want a story or he was on that TV series *Total Control* – even my boys call him Hollywood,' she said, with a laugh.

Keri's mum was a hairdresser. Her dad was a builder. But all she wanted to be was a cowgirl. She saved enough money to work on a ranch in America and then came back to North Queensland and worked on big properties a long way from nowhere, mustering and bore-running, and when she was pregnant and her belly was too big to start the pumps she became the station's cook. That's what she was doing the night her first son, Clancy, was born two months early. She'd defrosted pickled pork by mistake for the 20 workers so she'd grabbed leftover roast and made gravy, and then her waters broke. There was panic. They weren't prepared for a premature baby.

The Royal Flying Doctor Service arrived just in time to deliver Clancy. The property manager and their workers raced against the clock to line the airstrip with burning kerosene rags so the plane and its tiny patient could get on its way safely to Cairns Hospital. There was no humidicrib onboard and Keri held an oxygen mask over her tiny baby's face, his body wrapped in a towel, for the two hours to Cairns. It was 2am when they landed and he was rushed to the special care baby unit. When she was eventually able to leave Cairns with her new son two months later, Keri did the nine-hour drive back to the property by herself.

When she told Steve a few years ago that she wanted to learn how to train a dog, no one was going to argue. She's building up her team. She's got Leroy Brown and Bobby McGee. Bobby replaced Maggie May, who'd been her favourite until a snake got her. Bobby McGee's got a lot of presence but not a lot of confidence. She'll work on it, and a few cheeky barbs from Steve along the way are nothing compared to what she's been through.

Steve has always had dogs, but it was only after the accident that his interest became more serious. 'What we like about the animals is that they don't lie,' he told me. 'It only takes a little bit of putting in and they give you so much more back and it's pretty enjoyable.'

We were at Steve's home in the back streets of Winton, a few blocks from the pub where he'd played pool against Keri's young son, Harry, the night before. It wasn't yet lunchtime but it was already hot and we were debating if the temperature was going to hit 37 later or if that was tomorrow's forecast. It reminded me of my stint living in North Queensland for my first job in television back in 1992. The newspaper I'd been working for in Brisbane had suddenly closed down just before Christmas and I'd taken one of the first jobs on offer. I'd never been north of the Tropic of Capricorn let alone lived there, and I was told two things I've never forgotten: beer would always be served in a stubby holder and I'd be regretting my decision not to buy an air-conditioned car.

The heat is more serious for Steve because he's lost the ability to regulate his body temperature. He's always hydrating, and he keeps a fire extinguisher filled with water in the buggy in the shed and uses that to spray himself. When I asked him how he knows he's overheating, he answered by shutting his eyes and slumping his head to the side.

He spends hours welding branding irons in the shed, a hobby that quickly took on a professional aspect. He's now booked up for months in advance with requests coming in from big cattle companies and small enterprises. Sometimes it will be a newly registered brand as a gift for a child who's been given their first calf on a family property.

But it's the dogs that dictate the rhythm of his day. His uncles all had dogs – border collies – and they worked his grandfather's two properties of 14,000 sheep. When I visited Steve in Winton there were about 25 dogs out the back in cages, including about a dozen puppies from two separate litters. Some were just weeks old. Steve was planning on selling a few of the older, already trained dogs at an auction the following weekend. He's got his own cattle on a mate's property out of town and a few sheep in a yard behind his house, enabling him to work and train the dogs. He enjoys competing in dog trials and won't take a dog along until they've worked for him at home.

'A lot of people think, *Oh, it's just a trial dog, and they don't know how to work because we only work three sheep in the competition*, but three head of sheep is the hardest to hold together. I'd rather work two hundred any day before three head.'

He loves the training, watching the young ones learn and trying to develop a genetically improved line of dogs. Taking on the extra duties of a puppy for *Muster Dogs* wasn't necessarily on his wish list and he wasn't wedded to some of the milestones Neil McDonald was setting or convinced about the 12-month timespan.

'It all depends on the dog, how intelligent and how well he's bred, but the dog will tell you mostly. They really start maturing at two years old so you can really see a difference after that.'

Steve's had a mix of breeds over the years, border collies or kelpies or a cross of both, and was happy to have a little grey and white border collie he called Indi as part of the *Muster Dogs* experiment. The first thing he looked for in Indi was whether she had a natural ability, a sign she wanted to get to work and start herding while keeping a calm mind. He wasn't counting on her being so wilful. 'She's a real gem but I'm not sure if she has decided she's gonna work with me yet.'

I'd turned up with the film crew to watch Steve put Indi through her ten-month assessment. The paddock we were using was at his friend's place, Oondooroo Station, originally a sheep farm, now a cattle property with deep ties to Banjo Paterson. They say it's where he first performed 'Waltzing Matilda'. Before we could begin filming, we had to clear the paddock of a couple of nervous horses. Steve watched them and said quietly, 'They'll head to that open gate down there in a couple of minutes.' I couldn't even see an open gate but, sure enough, the horses calmed down, dropped their necks and ambled over to the gate. Steve had read their mood.

Two rams who were still hanging around needed a bit more encouragement and Steve zipped off on his Segway-modified chair across the rough terrain to move them on. I followed, thinking I could help. As I held my arms out to the sides saying, 'I'll block them, hey Steve?', he looked at me dismissively and with a shake of his head moved them on himself, a gentle reminder of what Keri first told me: Steve can be obstinately independent.

When we finished filming that day, we were dusty and sweaty and it was time to let the dogs out for a run. It hadn't ended up hitting 37 degrees but had got close enough. Steve's energy levels were starting to flag, so we flopped in chairs under a tree and Keri handed out beers – in a stubby holder, of course. I let out a sigh as the cold sensation hit the back of my throat.

'I bet that tastes like an angel's pissed on your tonsils, hey?' Keri said over her shoulder with a big laugh as she headed off to finish the yard work. The whirring of Steve's wheelchair told us he hadn't bothered waiting. Even at the end of a long hot day of filming, he was back on the job.

*

The weather can play havoc for our *Muster Dogs* participants. Their canine workmates still need to be fed and given a run. And the jobs won't wait. That was all on Zoe Miller's mind as she inched her truck along a highway just a couple of hours before midnight.

She had three horses and eleven dogs onboard and with the rain coming down steadily she was taking it slow. The 25-year-old had come from her home in Katherine in the Northern Territory and was heading to Augathella in Queensland, a few days' drive depending on how many breaks she took.

'I knew the heavy rain was going to be an issue, so I got on the road three days earlier,' Zoe told me a few months later, when I spoke to her on the phone for the first time.

Just out from the Queensland border, with the water running across the Barkly Highway and no moonlight to help, she saw the dark patch of a washout too late. It was deep, and even though she'd only been doing 20 kilometres an hour she thought the rough hole in the road might have done some damage. She stopped and flicked on the hazard lights before doing a lap of the truck as the rain belted down. It all seemed okay, but another driver who'd pulled up suggested she wait it out till first light; it was too dangerous to keep driving, they reckoned.

'I got up at 4am, packed up the dogs and the horses and hit the road again,' Zoe told me. 'I got past Soudan, where the water was meant to be bad, and I thought, *Awesome, I'm past it all.* I was driving along, had the music going and then I came to a hill and could see all the trucks lined up in the distance; between us, water.'

She spent a day and a half stranded 'with the Barkly winds rocking the truck' and then another four days stuck near Camooweal, until the town started running short of food and the conga line of trucks and road trains were escorted through.

The true scale of the catastrophic Gulf floods of early 2023 wouldn't be known for months. Tens of thousands of livestock were destroyed, residents were airlifted to safety and critical infrastructure was damaged.

Zoe Miller is a woman on a mission, fed by a deep well of

family history that makes her a sixth-generation cattlewoman. Her great-grandfather Blake Miller drove cattle for Sir Sidney Kidman, who earned the nickname 'The Cattle King' for his prominence as a pastoralist and entrepreneur in the late nineteenth and early twentieth centuries. In 1904 Miller became the first person to bring a thousand head of cattle safely across the 240-kilometre Murranji Track, a stock route dreaded for its thick scrub and lack of water. It was known as the ghost road of drovers.

With this kind of heritage, flooded roads across inland Australia in the twenty-first century weren't going to rattle Zoe, even if she was going it alone.

'Did you ever, at some point near midnight when the rain was pouring down and you had all these animals on an impassable road, did you ever question your life choices?' I asked her, prodding for any signs of vulnerability.

She did not. 'It's just one of the challenges you face,' she replied.

On that flood-delayed trip from Katherine, with hours to kill, Zoe contemplated what was ahead. She'd taken a month-long contract to educate 1600 Angus-cross weaners on a property just out of Augathella.

The graziers employ her to start working with the young cattle who have been weaned from their mothers. While Zoe teaches new skills to the weaners, the graziers are busy mustering the breeder cows. It can be a long process on those huge cattle stations, so having a skilled contractor like Zoe to begin educating the weaners makes a big difference.

'I usually have four to five days to work these fresh weaners through my program,' she said, 'and by the end I'm handing back these animals who are calm and easy to handle, whether it be in the yards or out in the paddock. Before they're weaned, these young animals have always been led to food and water by their mothers out in the paddock. So now it is my job to teach them how to graze and walk calmly to water.'

She enjoys it because she sees the gains for the business she's contracted to but also for animal welfare – 'it's such a win–win'.

Her dogs and horses are her companions on her long road trips between jobs, and she wouldn't want it any other way. After school, she'd been accepted to study nutritional science at university but took a gap year and never looked back. She was barely in her twenties when she took on a job as head stockwoman on one of Australia's most historically important livestock properties: Wave Hill, 500 kilometres south of Katherine, Northern Territory. Back in 1966, 2000 Gurindji stockmen, domestic workers and their families had walked off the station in protest about pay and working conditions. It was a decade before the dispute was resolved and the images of that time, of then prime minister Gough Whitlam pouring soil into the hands of Vincent Lingiari, remain etched into the storyline of Australia's First Nations history.

'There are a lot of gravesites and the old homesteads on the place, and I was able to connect parts of history together. When the locals come out from the communities – and we worked with a lot of them – they would tell us the stories of being a kid there and growing up in the old homestead. It's pretty amazing to see that and experience that with them.'

Zoe's father, Gavin, was managing the station and he had confidence his young daughter could step up. They had 40,000 head of cattle by the time the property was sold a few years later to an Australian family-led syndicate for a record $104 million. It's hard to comprehend the scale of what they were working with: 1.2 million hectares of some of the hardest land in the country. It was there Zoe truly understood what well-trained dogs could bring to the job.

'Finding people to work rurally has become harder over the years, and once I built up my own team of dogs there was no looking back,' she said. 'I would often have my crew say, "Oh thank goodness for your dogs." Or when I hadn't taken my dogs for a particular job: "Gee whiz, we really could have used their backup!"'

Her three older brothers, Blake, Robey and Matt, are proud of what she's done and often joke she's the 'favourite son' in the family. She's certainly determined to succeed in an industry where women are still in the minority. It's a far cry from her first nickname – 'Whoops' – earned when her mum became pregnant eight years after Matt was born.

'When Mum was in hospital having me, one of the Catholic primary schoolteachers asked Matthew where she was and he told her she was off having a "whoops",' Zoe told me with a laugh.

Zoe had watched the first series of *Muster Dogs* with her partner at the time, Mark. He'd been passionate about working horses and dogs on the land and he could turn his hand to just about anything. He'd left school at 15 and had barely spent a day not working. Together they had made plans to contract out their skills and keep doing what they loved. That's when Zoe saw the social media post calling for interest in a new series of *Muster Dogs*. Despite her outward confidence she baulked.

'I just thought, *Well, that's not for me.* It was too out there.'

For just a moment I got a glimpse of a young woman still finding her self-worth.

A month or so later she got a call from trainer Neil McDonald. He wanted her to think about joining the show. Mark and Zoe were both busy trying to build their business, often taking on separate contracts, keeping them apart for weeks if not months at a time. Would the added responsibility of taking on a *Muster Dogs* pup make things harder? Signing up for a TV show was definitely going to force Zoe out of her comfort zone. But Neil's suggestion to 'throw your name in the hat' opened a door in her head that she'd closed. 'Getting out of your comfort zone is always a good thing,' she said, 'and this was about a light-year out of my comfort zone!'

She'd worried how it would fit in with her work commitments but they'd offered to fly her new dog to Darwin and she'd meet the crew there. In the end, the two-month block of work she'd had locked in was cancelled at short notice, and she went to the Hudsons' farm instead.

'They flew me to Dubbo to pick up the puppy and I saw them all and immediately thought I'd love the one that was black and white. Buddy was the biggest of the lot and he had beautiful, kind eyes,' she said, remembering the moment Carolyn had walked out with the litter. 'My other first thought was he looked very similar to a beautiful collie dog, Boss, that I had lost in a work accident earlier in the year. Whilst they never replace your old dogs, I recognised Buddy was the universe's funny little nod to the mate I had lost.'

No surprises that Zoe has a lot of admiration for Joni Hall, the livestock handler from series one who slowly let us into her rugged and solitary work life. 'I'd love to spend some time with her and do a bit of work if she's open to it because you never stop learning,' she said.

That's where our chat ended. Zoe was off to pick up her Swiss friend Magalie, whom she'd met when they'd both worked at Wave Hill. They'd had an instant connection: Magalie was as committed to the care of the animals as Zoe was, and also had a high drive to keep learning. She'd returned to her family in Europe but was now on her way back to do another season on the land with Zoe.

'She just goes the extra mile and she's also such a wonderful friend and massive support,' Zoe told me. 'And it'll be good to have an offsider, for safety if nothing else. I mean a gate could fly back onto me and no one would know if I'm in the yards alone,' she admitted, showing just a hint of acknowledgement that this is no easy path she's chosen.

It's the kind of relationship built on camaraderie, trust and respect – out amid the challenges and rough beauty of the vast Australian landscape.

*

All of our participants – Steve, Lily, Russ, Cilla and Zoe – would be drawing on their different sources of strength and support as they began their journeys to turn their new companions into working dogs, and knowing each of their triumphs and disappointments would be shared with a global audience.

CHAPTER 3

Feeding the Nation

They're a varied mob, our *Muster Dogs* participants. Some leapt at the chance to be on the television show while others, like Steve, needed convincing along the way that they'd made the right decision. What they share is a love of the country and we've had a glimpse at the reasons they're doing it.

But you might be asking yourself – especially if you're a city-dwelling non-dog-owner – 'Why should I care about this?'

Let me take you on a tangential trip, behind the studio doors of breakfast television, to give you a bird's-eye view of the unseen chains of information that link us all.

There are some mornings on ABC *News Breakfast* when we're just not sure where three hours of live programming will take us. A lot of it depends on the news of the morning and what's happened overseas while we've been asleep. When my alarm goes off at 3am, I quickly scan the breaking news alerts, expecting anything from disasters to the deaths of dictators. We have some interviews locked in the night before by producers who knock off around midnight, and we will have the celebrity chats that are often booked weeks in advance to give us the time to watch the about-to-be-released blockbuster or listen to the new music release or whatever it is that's motivated a household name to get up at sparrow's fart to appear on national television.

As presenters, our minds are pinged from politics to pleasure to puns like a ball in a pinball machine, from one minute to the next during the wild three-hour ride of live television, and it's difficult to shake the pattern of working like this. Which is probably why, in the process of writing that last paragraph, I went down a rabbit hole of research to check that 'sparrow's fart' is appropriate language in this book. I always thought sparrow's fart was Australian slang but, thanks to British language expert Paul Anthony Jones, I've now learned the expression first appeared in an 1828 dictionary in North Yorkshire in the United Kingdom, where they know a thing or two about early mornings and sparrows. They actually defined it as 'three hours before daylight'.

The point is, each morning on *News Breakfast* we never quite know where conversations are going to lead. We prepare by having a head full of stories and anecdotes. And sparrow's fart may well turn up in my chat one morning now that I've discovered its origin. And then there's the unexpected technical glitch, where you have to call on all your experience to make sure the viewers don't detect something's gone awry in the control room and that everyone behind the camera is scrambling. It's a little unnerving when the autocue goes to black, for example, and is suddenly devoid of script or direction. These are the moments where you're adlibbing on a subject you hadn't anticipated just minutes before.

The equipment we use to connect to our reporters in the regions is beyond anything I could have imagined when I started in Townsville in the early 1990s, reporting throughout the north and west of Queensland. If we wanted to send footage of interviews to Brisbane for that night's 7pm news, we'd go to the local Telecom exchange, find an external metal box and plug in our camera cables, call the intake desk at the ABC in Brisbane and make sure they were recording, and then sit in the dust while all our material was sent out in real time, frame by frame. We would often have the key to these boxes, but on Thursday Island in the Torres Strait, for example, we would have to wait until the Telecom employee arrived to open the box and grant us access. And if they were out fishing for the day, then you'd just try again the next day. Nothing happened fast enough for any of our colleagues in Brisbane, but patience was the first thing I learned working in the regions. Now reporters can send pictures and put themselves in front of a camera for a live cross within minutes thanks to the advancements in technology.

It's not failproof, though, and occasionally the signal will be too scratchy or we lose it altogether, and the output producer makes a snap decision to go to the next interview or story. Sometimes when news stories are breaking in real time and the autocue in front of us is blank, the output producer will offer the instruction in our earpieces to simply 'fill'. This is our cue to adlib, filling up the time as best we can while our producers secure the next interview and the control room can patch through the talent's video and audio stream. Early on during a breaking news event in the US when I was still learning the ropes on breakfast television, I thought I was following that direction with ease, repeating facts and putting the situation into context and filling the empty minutes on air. It was only after several increasingly insistent 'FILL!' directives in my ear that I realised the producer was actually saying 'Phil' and wanted me to cross to our reporter Phil Williams, who was on the streets of LA, waiting on the line for a live cross.

It was during one of those mornings when the other presenters and I were scratching for conversation that finance presenter Madeleine Morris revealed the dire straits in her household that had been caused by the great frozen chip shortage that had begun at the end of 2022. Potato harvesting and planting had been affected by a series of floods and there was little sign of supply returning to normal anytime soon. One of the big supermarket chains had put a limit on the number of bags of frozen chips customers could buy, while some fish and chip shops had tried substituting sweet potato chips or salad and rice. Those were choices that could be considered almost 'un-Australian', but that was the level of desperation to which they'd sunk. Madeleine said her young daughters weren't accepting her attempts to slice up actual potatoes and wanted the 'real' chips from the supermarket freezer.

It wasn't the first time we'd been chatting on the program about food shortages. We think of ourselves as living in a country with great food security but during the pandemic we discovered just how quickly supply chains could be disrupted (beyond the well-publicised and frequently mocked toilet roll shortage). Covid illness among workers in processing plants meant meat, including mince and chicken, was limited and at times shelves were left empty. And it probably won't be the last time either. There are predictions that drought, floods, heatwaves, bushfires, worker shortages and geopolitical ructions, as seen with the Ukraine war, will continue to challenge our farmers as they try to feed and clothe us for a reasonable cost.

You might be wondering how any of that relates to a television series about working dogs. Well, stick with me here. There have been many books written about Australia's rural industries, but the one with the most tantalising title is *Why You Should Give a F*ck About Farming*. It's a comprehensive assessment about farming in Australia, written by the respected journalist Gabrielle Chan. She was a city girl originally, born in Sydney after her dad, who was of Chinese heritage, migrated from Singapore. After years of reporting on state and federal politics, she married a farmer and moved to a sheep and wheat farm in country New South Wales. All of that gives her a really interesting insight into rural Australia. Her reasoning for why you should care is simple, although her analysis is detailed and thorough: it's because you eat. And before you say, 'But I don't eat meat,' read on.

'Many of us now use food as a marker for our values: carnivore, vegan, vegetarian, pescatarian, gluten-free, paleo,' she wrote in her 2021 book. 'We eat based on price, or our wish to mitigate climate change, or to have an effect on land regeneration, local producers or the price of milk.'

Her argument is that there is no delineation between 'farmers' and 'others'. If you eat or wear clothes, the decisions you make can and do influence farming. She says eaters will be the ultimate arbiter for where and how food is grown, and that everyone has a stake in the future of food and agriculture.

Despite the pressure of her daily writing job for *The Guardian* and book projects, Gabrielle is generous with her knowledge and has taken more than a few calls from me over the years when I've found myself creatively stuck. No matter what chaos might be raining down on her, she answers her phone in a soft, slow voice, appearing to have all the time in the world for me. And so it was again when I gave her a call as I began writing this book. We nattered about her grandkids and the revelation she's finally succumbed to taking up baking late in life, before we launched into a long conversation about what's happening in rural Australia and how the vast population that hugs the coastline and fills our cities views the country. Her logic is sound; because we are all consumers in some way, we need to take a greater interest in what's going on in the nation's farms.

And it's the same logic that motivated most of our participants to take part in *Muster Dogs*, even if they began their journey to television stardom with a little reluctance. In one of my earliest chats with Frank Finger, I asked him what he thought was the most important thing about what he did for a crust. His answer? Feeding the nation.

'We're just one little part, but it doesn't matter how big or how small you are, we're all needed in the grazing industry,' he told me on the phone from the farmhouse where he lives with his wife, Cathy. 'We try to breed a beast that the meatworks will want and the buyers will want.'

The Fingers, with their long history in the region, have re-evaluated the kind of cattle they should run on their property over the years. The rough country of central Queensland is suited to Brahmans, which were first introduced to Australia from Texas in the 1930s and whose genetics can now be found in about 50 per cent of the national beef herd.

'We decided to cross the Brahmans with the Simmentals to put softness and growth into our male cattle, and that seems to have worked well. They sell well for us, they eat well and buyers just keep coming back for them.'

Frank and his family are always trying to improve what they're offering the market, but their greatest concern is being able to keep up supply. Before the first season of *Muster Dogs* went to air, Frank was concerned that Australian cattle herd numbers were down because of the drought in so many places, including in Western Australia where graziers, like fellow participant Aticia Grey, had taken the drastic action of completely destocking their properties. Restocking and getting animals back to prime condition doesn't happen overnight and the supply chain gets a jolt because of it. Frank, on the other hand, had enjoyed some good seasons and he wanted to make sure he kept contributing.

'We don't want meat to become too dear for the consumers, and not everything goes overseas. We've got to feed Australians and if it becomes too expensive, that worries me and I'm worried that could be happening now.' Those were prescient words from Frank back in 2020, long before we knew about the impact of the Covid virus on supply chains, the hit to the economy and the subsequent cost-of-living crisis.

Around 90 per cent of what we eat is grown domestically – by people like Rob Tuncks on his property, Lazy Acres, where he and his wife farm around 1000 sheep on 600 hectares, or Cilla Pershouse on her property in southeast Queensland, or by farmers on the properties where Joni Hall and Zoe Miller educate cattle.

The head of the Australian Bureau of Agricultural and Resource Economics and Sciences (ABARES), Dr Jared Greenville, puts it this way: 'All the stuff that happens outside of cities is really responsible for putting food on the table for the average Australian.'

Jared had always been 'that kid' in school, the one who loved maths and economics, who was fascinated by why things play out in a certain way and why people act in a particular way. Gabrielle suggested I talk to him to help connect *Muster Dogs* viewers and readers of this book to what's happening on the land right now.

ABARES is the research division of the federal Agriculture Department and Jared's job is to keep across the forecasts and data. It all happens at Agriculture House – a government building whose name, I imagine, was the result of endless brainstorming meetings with well-paid consultants. Thankfully, the work that goes on inside the Canberra headquarters is considered unique – and a lot of it happens in Jared's office. It's tucked to the side of the otherwise open-plan floor and doubles as a meeting room; its walls are soundproofed with just enough space to hang a well-used whiteboard.

Teams of researchers and analysts pore over hundreds of sets of data: trade, price, climate, whatever they need to forecast what's happening with each section of the agriculture industry. They don't rely simply on feeding the data into models to produce the work – a method Jared says has led to 'horribly wrong' forecasts in the past.

'They talk to people, a whole range of stakeholders who know the sector and who have a real sense of what's going on amongst all the data and noise,' Jared told me. And that's why when he releases the official forecasts each year, he's confident the forecasters have done everything they can to make them as accurate as possible. They'll try to predict how much grain or beef, for example, will be produced and what the markets will pay for it, taking into account factors like climate and global stability.

Knowing and understanding what's ahead on the land will help people make the changes they need to when it comes to work practices and culture. For instance, did you know that 55 per cent of Australia's total landmass is taken up by agriculture? That's a huge chunk once you take out the rest of us in the cities and the bits that are unforgiving desert.

'From a stewardship aspect – from maintaining the environment, from dealing with pests and weeds and ecosystems – farmers do a lot of work in that regard,' he told me. 'When we talk about things happening on farms, we're talking about what's going on across a broad swathe of the country and that's important for everyday lives. Things that farmers have changed and got better at directly influence people's livelihoods. For example, we don't get those big dust storms like we used to get that would come rolling into cities and we've seen improvements in the health of our river systems.'

Muster Dogs gave us a close-up look at some of those incredible landscapes. There are two extreme seasons in the Northern Territory – wet and dry – and they dictate how CJ and Joe farm. During the dry they won't see rain for six months, which is why the wet season, when it comes, is critical for replenishing the land, waterways and aquifers.

'Having a 1200-millimetre average rainfall during the wet season means that we can do things like hay production and put in improved pastures and also fatten cattle,' CJ explains. Farming in the Top End is different from other parts of Australia, where you're not always sure when or if it's going to rain. 'Having a wet season means you know it's going to rain, it's just a matter of when.'

In November, ahead of the wet, they buy more young cattle to put on their property, Garabaldi, and then try to destock at the start of the dry season. It's the type and scale of hard work that would astound most of us in our easier city lives.

'It's just a continued rotation of grazing and that's to keep on top of any erosion, looking after your pastures, making sure there's not an overgrowth of pastures, because you can squash feed as well, so we're keeping an eye on our pastures,' CJ says.

The family's days are very different season to season. In the wet, they only work outside in the mornings and afternoons, moving the cattle during the cool hours of the day. In the middle of the day, when the heat is stifling, they focus on administration for the farm or you might find them in the workshop. They shift their cattle every three days or so to make the most of their paddocks.

'I don't believe farming is sustainably difficult. There are lots of people that have gone before us, teaching us how to do things properly and we can learn off those people,' CJ says. 'We put up fence lines so our cattle aren't damaging the banks of the Daly River and we do certain things like not overuse our water, or we don't use it to irrigate a crop that's not going to be viable, and we also look after our soils. Our soils are very important to us as farmers; we can't fatten cattle or grow crops without our soil.'

If you're still not convinced, here are some facts that show how important all this is: in 2023, Australia's rural industries were on track to produce a record $90 billion, thanks to high commodity prices, the war in Ukraine and the difficulties other countries were facing with drought. In the years when Covid shut down other industries like tourism and international education, agriculture kept people in jobs, bringing in income for export, freight and logistics workers as well as those directly working on the land.

Trying to work out what the future holds is where things get tricky. Rob Tuncks reckons the current generation has never known what it's like to suddenly not have an easy supply of food.

'The generation now has never gone hungry, the baby boomers never went hungry – and no one thinks you can go hungry, but if you actually look at what's happening with the supply and demand for food, we're not going to keep up with the growing population.' Rob's decision to leave his corporate job in his early thirties was partly down to his interest in food supply.

'I saw it as an opportunity to be in an industry that was a safe place to be because we're going to be producing the food of the future and it had potential for growth.'

When Jared Greenville, the boss at ABARES, was a kid, he spent all his holiday time at his grandparents' farm, Dunedoo, near Dubbo, New South Wales. Jesse and Arthur Wicks had spent their lives building up the Merino sheep farm, but as the years went on and they struggled through the collapse of the wool reserve price scheme and got hit by drought, things got tough. By the time Jared was a 20-year-old university student studying agricultural economics, the family farm was losing money. One of his assignments required him to do a whole-farm plan so he chose Dunedoo as the case study. He studied gross margins in the region and cattle prices and told his grandparents if they switched to Angus and Murray Grey cattle and cut back the sheep there was money to be made. They took a punt on their uni student grandson and it paid off.

Decades on, Jared remains just as passionate about the work he does, but there's one area he can't confidently predict – the impact of climate change. We've heard the way people have tried to explain the enormity of what we've witnessed over the last few years, saying things like 'it's a once-in-a-hundred-year flood' or 'we haven't seen bushfires like that in 50 years'. But Jared says we need to stop using language like this because it has no relevance anymore. No matter how much historical data his team can gather, it's no longer a reliable predictor of what's ahead.

'The historical record is not what the next fifty or one hundred years will look like. We know there is going to be a significant amount of change. We're seeing it already with a concertina effect where the extremes of weather are greater and they're happening more frequently.'

He points to what's already happening on the land as a good sign: less clearing, less reliance on machinery, smarter ways of operating, and shifting to renewables and regenerative farming. He reckons rural Australia is closer to the longed-for carbon neutral farming than they're given credit for.

One of our series two participants, Lily Davies-Etheridge, is part of that conversion from traditional to regenerative farming. Her family property hugs the Darling–Baaka River for 25 kilometres east of Wilcannia in outback New South Wales. Lily's mum, Mog, opens it up for field days during which like-minded landowners can meet. These people are committed to moving beyond entrenched practices of the past, when inputs were heavy-handed and the environment was something they had to try to overpower rather than work with.

'I have a sense of responsibility about the land, and it's been very depleted over the last hundred years or so,' Mog told me after a day spent breaking in some horses for a friend. The Dorper sheep she breeds can be hard on the land so she's building more fencing and better managing the way they graze. 'People say, "Ooh, it just hasn't rained," or "There's been terrible floods, there's nothing we can do," but actually there are things you can do, for example, rotate stock so paddocks are resting.'

That approach to grazing is something trainer Helen McDonald knows well: she has been doing it for about 20 years. On a Sunday morning, when most of us are still contemplating what we're going to do with our day, Helen will already have been out in the paddocks shifting sheep. And it was no different when I spoke to her in April 2023. It had been a foggy start to the day when she'd pulled on her ankle-high gum boots. It was mild but she'd layered up, four layers, in fact, and a scarf. Helen and her husband, Neil, as you know, are two of Australia's leading dog educators and stalwarts of the *Muster Dogs* series. But they're also farmers and, with Neil away for long periods with his dog schools, Helen's the one looking after the property.

They have around 500 ewes on their 450 hectares in Keith, South Australia, and Helen moves them every day across 60 different paddocks. Each of the paddocks is called a cell. You might have heard of the term 'cell grazing', but don't let it constrain your imagination. In reality, each cell is about the size of a dozen football fields strung together. They're rectangular in shape, with a gate at each end. If the ewes have started the morning gathered together near one gate, it might only take half an hour to shift them into their next paddock. And if they're not, well, it can be a 1.5-kilometre walk and a lot more time to get them through. Rather than separate the ewes into different mobs, Helen keeps them all together so that she can give each paddock a longer rest. This way she doesn't need to put sheep back onto it to feed for two to three months.

'It means we can better manage those more fragile areas and by keeping livestock off it in the late summer, early autumn, when you're not getting a lot of rain, you can allow that country to rest up and not create erosion,' she told me.

The alternative is traditional grazing where animals remain in a paddock for long periods of time. 'What happens there is that animals will keep going back to the same plant for food and eventually it just won't grow any more or it will stop sending out seeds so you start losing the diversity you have on the property.'

Helen can count on one hand how many days off she's had in the past year, so it does require commitment. You can't plan on a weekend away unless you can get someone to come in – someone with the skills to treat your livestock in the same way as you do. It's hard to get your head around it, right? But it's worth being able to picture it for later when we talk about why farmers choose to use dogs over other farming techniques.

When Russ Fowler from Tasmania learned about cell grazing, he was quickly convinced about its benefits. He's got the largest landmass of all the participants in series two, as well as the most stock, and he puts huge expectations on himself to not only work the land but improve it.

'Cell grazing was developed from watching the wildebeest migrating across savanna plains in Africa and the effects of large numbers of animals on the grasses they grazed,' Russ explained on a video chat one day, while four-year-old Charlie played on the floor just out of sight. 'It's about giving big rest periods to areas of paddock to improve your ground cover. Imagine the paddock was a circle and the water source was in the middle, and you'd split it up like a pizza with electric fences and then the mob would move between the wedges like the wildebeest move between savannas.'

Cell grazing is part of his ambition to bring low-stress animals to market. Yes, they're destined for slaughter, but the farmers in our *Muster Dogs* series want you to see the priority they give to the animals' welfare up to that point.

It's a key element of future success for farmers. Consumers are increasingly demanding higher standards of welfare; the 2020 Meat Industry Strategic Plan found that the demand for higher standards of animal welfare was the single biggest factor in making sure a farm product would find a place in the market.

And Rob Tuncks, with the perspective of a man whose previous life was in the corporate money-making world, says there's a simple reason why 100 per cent of the focus on his farm is on animal welfare: economics.

'That's the whole business of this farm. The end goal is to have healthy, fat lambs to sell and healthy breeders to keep. You spot them the best feed you can, and you handle them the best way that you can.'

Rob was deeply interested in what was happening on the land long before he decided to ditch his day job and go farming. His dad was a senior lecturer at Roseworthy Agricultural College, now part of the University of Adelaide. Rob moved to the city after school, but he always had that connection with friends and relatives on the land.

'Farmers want to look after the landscape and they want to look after their livestock, and you get the odd bad apple, but you can't mistreat your livestock and land and expect it to be productive for twenty or thirty years,' he said, arguing the case for all of us to have more respect for what's going on in country Australia.

Rob feels like he's learned a thing or two over the 20 years he's been farming but he'll readily admit missteps along the way. 'When I first bought this place, the mistakes were costing us a lot of production because I didn't know enough.' Early on after their move to the farm, Rob endured a lot of lambs dying from worm infestations. He didn't know, as a newcomer, to watch out for a high worm count because the wet weather had led to prolonged periods of lush green grass through summer.

Mistakes like this often take 12 months to fix because you're working on an annual cycle as a farmer. 'If you're programming a computer or doing some coding and you make a mistake and you figure out there's a better way to do it, the very next time you touch that keyboard you've improved yourself and you've stepped it forward. I said this to an old farmer who was in his eighties – I said, "Look, I've been doing this for fifteen years and I still don't think I know anything," and he said, "I've been doing it for sixty and I still feel the same way."'

The concept of cell grazing and building paddocks with electric fencing works for some of our participants, but what about for someone like Aticia Grey in Western Australia?

'Our country is not really set up for intensive fencing. There are a lot of hills, a lot of mountains, a lot of hard country,' she told me. 'I would probably like to concentrate more on the stock behaviour side of things.'

Aticia, as one of the 30 per cent of women who work properties in Australia, is keen to have Glenflorrie, her family's immense property in the Pilbara, at the forefront of the move to regenerative agriculture.

'It's what's under the soil instead of just focusing on what's above it – it's your microbes and your organisms and it's the ecosystem as a whole, including the people and all the animals in it, and it gives you a whole new perspective including your wild dogs and your dingoes, they're part of the whole ecosystem.'

She's been looking at something called 'instinctual migratory grazing', which resets the instincts of the livestock, so they behave more like the buffalo herds used to as they crossed North America, staying as one mob to come in and graze, and then moving on to cover new country. She's excited about what the future holds, and what her family's property has the potential to be.

Everyone on the land is facing challenges of some sort: the uncertainty of climate change and international export markets, the cost of fertiliser or getting a tractor fixed, having enough staff for a successful harvest. But our *Muster Dogs* participants all share a common approach – and Neil

McDonald, our dog trainer, sees it whenever he holds his schools. 'We're in control of how we work our livestock, so that's the one area that people can take on and manage and get to a higher level without being controlled by outside forces that are out of their hands.'

No one ever said farming was easy. My four siblings and I have a WhatsApp chat group that can sometimes go days without being roused from its sleep. But every now and then we'll land on questions or subjects that generate long conversations that go on until I'm forced to mute the phone and head to bed.

While writing this book, I've been sending them regular questions, checking on our own family history on the land. My older siblings – Robert and David, who are now in their seventies, and Wendy, the youngest of the three – clearly remember those early days of Mum and Dad's dairy farming life; they were all expected to pitch in. Wendy reminded us of the Sundays we'd spend visiting family friends on a nearby cattle property in Kilkivan. The adults would play on the antbed tennis court – created, as the name suggests, from the mounds of earth left behind by ants, that were rolled and crushed to create a flat playing surface – and Wendy said it would be a treat if she was allowed to pick up a racket and join them. It felt like Christmas. But then as other families settled in for the afternoon on the classic country house veranda, Dad would call stumps early with the familiar call: 'Righto, kids, let's go. We have cows to milk.' It was the twice-a-day job of a dairy farmer, even with machines doing a lot of the work. Twice a day. Seven days a week.

We've spoken a lot over the years of the attempts Mum and Dad made to improve the way they farmed and lived. They worked with agronomists on the paddock designs on the sloping land and, in the 1960s, built contour or deviation banks to slow water flows and stop erosion. Whenever our family got together when my parents were still alive, 'Dad's Deviation Banks' would come up in conversation, pretty much without fail. He was that proud of them.

But it struck me that in all those conversations I'd never asked my older brothers if there'd ever been an expectation they'd return home from boarding school and take over the farm on Running Creek Road.

'Dad had no chance in hell of me going farming,' David wrote back immediately when I posed the question to them on our chat. He worked as a labourer and then became a successful landscaper.

'I would feel homesick at times at boarding school, and I missed all of what living in the country offered,' Robert, who went on to become a banker, chimed in. 'I'd raised with Dad the prospect of coming onto the farm and his response rings loudly in my ears to this day. "No, Rob, you can do better in life than the farm." And the rest is history.'

As an afterthought I followed up with a question for Wendy: 'I suppose it wasn't even considered at the time that a daughter would take over the farm?'

'You got that right!' she messaged back. 'I guess riding out to check boundary fences doesn't equate to running a farm.'

She'd played an important role in the family work dynamics. They all had. But Dad's response to Robert wasn't a reflection of any lack of regard for farming. Far from it. Mum and Dad had left public service jobs in Sydney after Dad's World War II service to follow a dream to be farmers. They were the first and last generation of their families to work with livestock on the land.

No, Dad's advice for Robert would have been driven by an acknowledgement that life on the farm – their life at least – had been tough, the days long, the weather challenging and the profits small.

So much has changed now, and we've seen it on the properties of our *Muster Dogs* participants. Technological advancements and a wealth of knowledge are available at our fingertips with the tap of a keyboard. It feels almost counterintuitive then, in this new century, that farmers are making progress by turning back the clock and finding new appreciation for the natural instincts and trained skills of their four-legged partners.

CHAPTER 4

Kelpies versus Collies

About five minutes into the trip to the Fowlers' sheep paddocks in central Tasmania, I make my first mistake. I'm sitting in the front of the ute with my neck twisted towards the back to face Rosie, who is telling me a story about the farm's history while also trying to calm her crying ten-month-old daughter, Milly. Her husband, Russ, pulls on the handbrake and jumps out of the driver's seat to open a gate, and as he swings it wide and sprints back to the car, it dawns on me: I've failed Farm Etiquette 101.

There are two unassailable rules on farms: leave gates the way you find them; and if you're the front passenger you jump out quick to be the one to open them. Russ puts the ute into 4WD to start the climb up a rocky hill and waves off my apology. 'All good, you get the next one,' he says.

'Don't worry about it,' Rosie chimes in from the back. 'When Milly was born and we had both the kids in the buggy, I'd always sit between them and say, "I'm in the middle, I can't get there."' And she has a giggle dobbing in her father-in-law: 'John is so naughty, he's always saying, "I'll just be a second, I'll come back through this way" to avoid having to close them.'

I have no 'middle seat exemption' excuse and, anyway, I want to prove my worth as a farmhand, so as gate after gate appears I've got the car door open and half a leg out before the ute's even stopped. On a couple of occasions Russ offers a helpful instruction as we approach: there's a half-moon lock that needs to line up perfectly with its other matching half to open, and then there's an electric bungie gate that requires wrestling with the pull of the elastic without getting zapped. Thankfully there are more than a couple of simple hook latches, which I seem capable of handling, even if there never seems to be quite enough chain.

'Farmers are always tight with the amount of chain they give you; it's only just enough,' Rosie jokes.

As we set off again Russ reminds her that gates have got to be tight to stop sheep squeezing through, that's the whole point. By the time we get to a gate that is secured to three others, all with their own locks, at a point where four paddocks meet, I'm ready to call it quits.

'How many bloody gates have you got on this place, Russ?' I ask incredulously as I'm fiddling with this Rubik's Cube version of fencing.

'At least I haven't given you a cocky's gate,' Russ calls from behind the wheel.

Actually, I might have been able to manage that one. I remember the cocky's gate from my childhood, although when I remind my sister Wendy about it a few days later, she groans. They were the simplest home-made gates but often the hardest to open or close. You'd sit the pole on one side of the fencing into a loop of wire at the bottom of the gatepost and then use your muscles to pull the top of the gate towards the fence post and secure it with a bit of wood that you'd use as a lever to lock it in place.

'It was great when you got it locked in,' she says. And then we remember the trick to opening it: slowly releasing the tension off the metre-long bit of wood you were using as a lever, just enough so you could take the fence pole out of the loop of wire but not so quickly that you got an almighty whack as the tension released and the piece of wood flung back at you.

This cheerful couple in their thirties have a bit of history with fences. Russ wooed Rosie when he was working on a property in Western Australia; she was the 'girl next door', living with her parents. Marriage and two children later, and with Rosie's cancer three years in remission, they're keen to think about the future. They've got about 18,500 sheep and 100 paddocks on their properties that they either own or lease, hence the number of gates. Russ says his dad was the innovator, separating the land into smaller paddocks to begin cell grazing. Russ is taking it up a notch, investing in electronic irrigation pivots with arches that span out across the paddocks like small versions of the Sydney Harbour Bridge. He hates it when critics suggest farmers aren't environmentally friendly.

'Does a shopkeeper not clean his shop? It's not in our interest by any stretch of the imagination to not look after what we've got. If we don't protect our waterways and if we don't keep good pasture cover on our paddocks it would have a devastating impact on our bottom line,' he says.

The other thing that makes it all work is his team of dogs.

Molly, our *Muster Dogs* border collie, is in the back of the ute on the day I visit, along with Chief, an eight-year-old huntaway, and Ted, a four-year-old kelpie, and they're busting to get to work. They're tired of the stop–start progress of our property tour and by the time we get to a paddock full of ewes they're desperate to jump out and round them up. I notice a lot of sheep have blue marks on their lower backs near their bottoms and I wonder out loud if they've already been marked for slaughter.

'Oh no, they're the ones we hope are pregnant,' Russ explains. The rams have a harness with a block of blue chalk strapped to them so when they mate with a ewe, the chalk rubs

Russ's automated irrigation pivots in Bothwell, Tasmania. (Richard Rowley)

Neil McDonald at CJ's property in Douglas Daly, Northern Territory. (Melissa Spencer)

against the ewe's rump, leaving a stain. I'm looking at a sea of blue – the animal world's version of the scarlet letter – but it gives Russ an easy way to determine who could be delivering a lamb in five months.

Chief and Ted do most of the work, moving through a semi-circle behind the sheep. Molly, who's less than a year old when I meet her, is still learning the trade. 'It's very rewarding as they grow up and hit different milestones and watching them *get* something for the first time,' Russ says. 'I just love my dogs and they're a part of me.' His dogs all have different personalities and different traits. 'They're like tools in a toolbox and you need to have lots of different tools to get the job done.'

Huntaways were originally bred as farm dogs in New Zealand, and Russ says his are pretty laid-back. 'They're quite happy to sit there and enjoy the day or they're quite happy to get in there and work. In heavily undulating country they're really good because they stand up on the top of the hill and they bark and the echo of the bark pushes the animals away from them. Hence, the name huntaway,' Russ explains. 'So they push them down to a fence or a creek and that will allow you to drive to a gateway or something like that.'

One of the benefits of working with dogs is that on steep hills you don't need to use a motorbike or a buggy and so you're avoiding occupational health and safety risks. Cutting down on the use of machinery has been one of the prime reasons many farmers are turning to working dogs. It's safer and cheaper and the stock are calmer.

Aticia Grey from series one found the transition to working with dogs so worthwhile that she'll readily say she'd rather work with them than a bigger team of people. 'As soon as you add machinery to the equation you're adding a lot more people around that you need to manage and I really like the idea of it just being a couple of us working, getting the job done with a couple of teams of working dogs,' she says from her home in Western Australia. She still needs to use helicopters for mustering on her enormous property (remember the length of that driveway?), but she'd like to do that less and less. It might take a little longer with dogs and she's okay with slowing the process down when she heads out to muster, especially when she sees the cost benefit. 'You don't have the cost of machinery, and diesel is not going to get any cheaper. So if we can pull our labour [costs] and our reliance on heavy machinery down, I really think it's going to improve our lifestyle; it's just going to make it more enjoyable.'

There's no way of knowing exactly how many working dogs there are in Australia. A report done for government organisation AgriFutures puts the number somewhere between 270,000 and 300,000. The same study revealed that dogs on sheep farms typically work for five hours a day, five days a week during the peak period of shearing, and they typically cover more than 40 kilometres a day, reaching speeds of up to

37 kilometres an hour. The researchers estimated that you get a 5.2-fold return on your investment in a good working dog.

Our tough cattlewoman Joni Hall from series one will take a dog over a human any day. 'People get distracted, but dogs are very focused on their job. I could love them all they like and say, "Good dog, love you," and pat them, but they really don't care, they just want to work,' she explains in her typically forthright way. 'You can't get staff like that, and they can't complain to HR because I *am* the human resources department. These dogs cost me about a thousand dollars a year [each] for their keep. They're quite resilient, they're not overly offended if you rouse on them, and they have a great effect on livestock.'

Many of the farmers and dog handlers I've spoken to believe a good dog is worth a couple of workers. But even if we settle on the equation that one dog can do the work of one human, that's a huge contribution from our four-legged workmates. Farmers face increasing costs and tough trade competition with other markets, and the price they're getting for their product can be out of their control at times. Getting a good dog and training it well can be a wise investment, especially if it helps with productivity.

CJ Scotney from series one remembers the first time she watched one man on his quad bike moving 1500 head of cattle with just his dogs. 'We were gobsmacked,' she says, explaining the moment she and her husband, Joe, decided that's how they wanted to run their property as well. 'The cattle were calm, the manager on his bike was calm, there was just no hoo-haa about it.' CJ uses her dogs to help rotate cattle through the dense scrub paddocks on their Northern Territory farm, and with the canine team she has, it's a job that can be done by CJ and Joe alone. 'We like to put those breeders in this thick bush country to keep the fuel load down so we don't get those hot fires through there that can really damage the flora and fauna. We couldn't get them in and out of there without the dogs.'

Farmer and dog trainer Helen McDonald has seen a lot of change in the industry over the decades and it hasn't necessarily all been good. Back in the day, mustering was done on horseback, but at a certain point horses were replaced by motorbikes and cars. 'The old guys that were shifting from mustering with horses to doing it with motorbikes and cars were doing it the same way they were doing it with their horses, basically with the motorbike moving at the same speed their horse would have been walking in the past.' She says sheep want to be mustered calmly and quietly and no farmer would want to see their livestock overheated and scared. 'But what's happened is you've got the generational change, and their grandkids get out on the bikes and they'll be just chasing the sheep, seventy or eighty kilometres an hour. They call it "brumby running". The livestock come in [to the yards] with dust in their wool, leaving their lambs behind and they're not right in the brain, and [farmers] have a lot of trouble moving them afterwards.'

Mustering with dogs rather than bikes or buggies makes the stock a lot calmer and that brings economic value to a property, but there's also the loyalty and companionship that working dogs offer their masters. We saw it with Joni in series one. She might have had some choice words for a few of her dogs at the end of a long hot day, but they were her mates as well through some lonely times. Russ in Tasmania was emotionally numb during the months Rosie was being treated for cancer, and his dogs could read him like a book. 'They pick up on all the little things, whether you're having a good day or a bad day,' he says. 'My dogs helped me because I could come home from visiting Rosie in hospital and go out and move a mob of sheep and they were instrumental in getting me through that with their loyalty and their commitment.'

That relationship between dog and human has been a constant on the land. I saw it time and again as a child. When my family moved from Kilkivan to Gympie, we left our beloved dog Mack in the care of Mum and Dad's best friends, the Fitzgeralds. They had originally started as dairy farmers and then moved into beef and began breeding Herefords. Carolyn was their youngest daughter and a playmate for Trudi and me and she loved dogs despite having had her face badly bitten as a three-year-old.

'I held a piece of bread out to the cattle dog and when it snatched it, I snatched it back and it bit me, all over my face,' she told me years later.

Her mum had rushed her to Gympie Hospital, a 40-minute drive away, and by the time she'd returned with her face taped up, the dog had been put down. It was devastating for all of them, especially her dad.

'You can't underestimate the relationship between a farmer and their dog,' she said. 'They're your colleague, your best friend, your confidante, your comforter. They provide a relationship that even humans can't and, to be honest, I think the farmers preferred the company of their dogs to some humans.'

When Carolyn was ten, the family lost three dogs in the space of a week to bait poisoning. It was so upsetting Carolyn was allowed to miss school, an extraordinary event, given that her mother so firmly believed in the value of education she had her husband teach their children how to safely cross swollen rivers so that flooded roads couldn't be used as an excuse for a day off. But that's how much these dogs mean to people in the country.

*

There are plenty of different farm dog breeds: the New Zealand huntaways that Russ Fowler owns; the energetic cattle dogs who might be a little smaller than other farm dogs but sure know how to use their size; and the beautiful white fluffy maremmas from Italy that Aticia Grey has in her mixed team.

But it's kelpies and collies that make up the majority of working dogs in Australia. Both breeds are intelligent, energetic and independent.

The first border collies were imported to Australia in 1900 from farms along the border of England and Scotland. Kelpies have been around a little longer, and the Victorian town of Casterton, population 1700, is considered their birthplace. Breeder, trainer and historian Nancy Withers tells the story of a young Irish bloke called Jack Gleeson, who in 1871 swapped a horse for a black and tan female pup he named Kelpie. The little dog came from the litter of a couple of different breeds of collies from Scotland and was the start of this new breed of Australian working dog. There has been debate over the years about whether kelpies interbred with dingoes, leading to some of them having yellow coats, but a University of Sydney study has ruled that out.

The pups in series one were all kelpies, whereas in series two they were border collies. So which is the better breed?

Our *Muster Dogs* trainer Neil McDonald puts it like this: 'What's better, a Holden or a Ford? Well, it doesn't matter which one it is, but it's the model. They used to say you didn't want a car made on a Monday morning or a Friday afternoon because on a Monday morning the workers might be hungover and on a Friday they're thinking about knocking off for the weekend, so you wanted the model made on a Wednesday. It's not whether they're kelpies or collies, it's the family line within the breed that's important.'

Regardless, Neil is less interested in where the dogs are from and more interested in where they're going. 'A lot of effort and energy and ideas and talk go into the dogs' origins. I reckon that same amount of effort needs to go into "How do we get these dogs going better?" People need to learn to talk to their dogs and not about their dogs.'

It's entertaining listening to the breeders and farmers describe the differences between collies and kelpies. Rob Tuncks turns to a car analogy as well. 'If your car is basically neat, all your tools are in the appropriate places and if you haven't got stuff on the floor and empty cans rolling around, you're probably more of a collie person. If your tools are sort of half-arsed and you cannot use the brake properly because there are beer cans getting stuck under the pedals, then you're probably more of a kelpie person. If you're like, "She'll be right, just do it your way, don't cause the stock any trouble, get to the right spots, don't bite, bark at the right times, just do it your way and I'll leave you alone," then that's a kelpie. So, kelpies generally don't like being told what to do very much. Whereas collies, you can boss them around, you can move them left, move them right, move them in; they love being told what to do. Some days I am a collie person and some days kelpie – that's why I have both.'

Mick Hudson, who with his wife, Carolyn, bred our border collie pups for series two, is a third-generation stockman and working dog trainer. He competes regularly in dog trials, where dogs and their handlers are put through their paces, moving livestock around a field and through various obstacles. The trials are designed to reflect what the dogs might face every day at work and to show off their skills. There's barely a competition in Australia Mick hasn't won and he's been the national champion several times. He says 90 per cent of dogs in the sport are border collies.

'Kelpies were developed over a time to suit the Australian conditions and they have a lot of natural ability and a lot of natural instinct and they were bred to do the job themselves but not to be educated to a higher standard,' he says. 'Some people find them ignorant, and it's not the kelpies' fault. They weren't bred for trainability or nature, they were bred to do the job.

'It's a good thing for dogs to train themselves in the paddock, but it's not real good when you're competing, and, because things are changing now, we're teaching people how to educate dogs to a higher standard, and the collie is more trainable and better natured and more of a pleasure to have around than a kelpie that's ignoring you.'

Okay, that's one for the collies. But remember, Mick is talking about competition work, and he does accept that kelpies make very good yard and farm dogs. 'But competition dogs? I struggle with them because they don't want to take a command,' he says.

Carolyn has had experience with both the kelpie and the collie and says the collies are more sociable and want to be near you more. 'They're happy to be with you and not running off and hiding,' she says.

Joe Spicer, our series one kelpie breeder, says he's been trying to breed kelpies that are more controllable and want to 'barrack for you and work with you'. He recalls a saying he's heard more than a few times: 'If you ask a collie to jump, it says, "How high?" – and if you ask a kelpie to jump, it says, "Why?" I love that kelpies do question you and don't just blindly follow fools. I love that they apply a bit of common sense and go, "Well, what's the purpose of that, mate?"'

I decide to ask Frank Finger, who won series one with his kelpie, Annie, whether he has a preference. Our chats often happen when Frank knows he's going to have a good phone signal for half an hour or so. This time he's on the road into Clermont to pick up a trainee worker who's going to stay overnight and give him a hand on the farm. As we discuss the kelpie versus collie question, there's a big pause down the line. I can hear the wind whistling through the gap in the window and the sound of the wheels on bitumen.

'Well,' he says, hesitating as he speaks, 'Annie is listening at the moment, so I'd have to say kelpie.'

Ever the diplomat, though, he quickly adds that he's had some lovely collies in his time and it depends what you need them to do. 'If you were competing in dog trials and wanted to have a dog that was more robotic, you'd go for a collie because kelpies don't like to be told what to do,' he says.

*

It is mesmerising to watch a well-trained muster dog in action. I can appreciate the way they sense their owner's desire, knowing exactly what to do with just an occasional simple direction. Stop. Back. Behind. It's all about the pressure and release. It's like a dance with one partner trying to convince the other that it's a backwards rumba not a waltz, but a dance in which the other partner might be a few hundred sheep or cattle or goats.

Rob says anyone can go out and chase livestock into yards with a dog, but it takes years to develop a rapport or a feel for them. 'You've got to have that sensitivity to what the livestock are thinking and not be too close so they're running, and you've got to be in the right place. If you're too far back, you're not having any impact and if you're too close they're running,' he explains. 'You've got to find that sweet spot and good dogs will do that; they find the sweet spot where you're applying pressure on the livestock and the livestock are responding in a way that's not frightening them.'

Training dogs is one thing; filming them in action requires another skill level entirely. Our camera operators on *Muster Dogs* had to learn enough about dog handling to understand the tasks the dogs were completing at each milestone test and be a step ahead of them to follow them through the viewfinder. Brad Smith, the DOP, describes a moment when he was using a super-long lens on his camera to get a tight shot of the eyes of a dog. 'It looked at the feet of the stock and then looked up to put pressure on the stock, just with its eyes, and back down again to take the pressure off the stock.'

As Brad describes how perfectly still the moment felt, I can picture it as if I was there.

'All of a sudden,' he says, 'something from around the back played up and the dog looked like it was moonwalking slowly – it took three steps away from the stock and took off around the back, looked like it smacked something around, then *woof, woof,* and he comes back and does the forward moonwalk, the last three steps in, into the same position, and lifts his eyes and looks up at the sheep as if to say, "I'm back."'

It's the combination of the mental calculations the dog is making alongside the physical endurance it needs that makes these animals so special. Neil McDonald has spent decades working in the industry and he is one of the experts best placed to explain the important role dogs can play on a farm. He has his own long history on the land to shape his understanding, having left school the day before he turned 15 to work on his father's farm in Keith, South Australia. It's about 250 kilometres from Adelaide and 500 kilometres from Melbourne. He was in his early twenties when his dad died, and he inherited the farm – and the debt that came with it.

'The debt on the place was greater than the value of the place, so that leads to a lot of get-rich-overnight schemes that don't always work. And it leads to a lot of off-property work in order to make enough money to develop it, shape it up and keep it going,' he reveals, being very honest about the realities he faced. When he and Helen got married, there was still plenty to be done to bring it up to scratch, to improve the pasture quality, to get the fencing right and have the proper water points for livestock. 'There are still areas that need brooming up a bit, but the work we've done has made it a good functional place.'

He praises Helen for having an addiction to stock buying and selling; depending on the season and the livestock prices, she can play it well. It was during some of his off-property work, like shearing and contracting, that Neil was first introduced to working dogs, and a career began to take shape: from getting a dog himself to having some early success working with dogs in the yards to demonstrating his developing skills at shows in places like Townsville and Cairns. People started asking him how to work a dog. 'And that's when I came up with the idea,' he says. 'Why don't we set up a course or a school where people come and learn to work dogs? At that point I thought it was just to train dogs. I didn't know that if you work dogs well, eventually the behaviour patterns of your livestock change, either for the better or the worse. If you handle dogs well, the cattle and sheep get easier every time.'

Neil rattles off a list of reasons why lifting the standard of dogs and the way they're handled is the key to a successful farm. 'We have a lot of trouble if our sheep and cattle don't want to come to us, if they want to run away, if they're always escaping from the mob, if the mob's scrumming, circling, peeling off – that makes it very hard to manage.'

His number-one reason is occupational health and safety. 'Dogs will help train the livestock to be nice and settled with cooperative behavioural patterns like walking up into a shearing shed.' He's seen people who get a rush of blood when the stock don't do what they want – they might jump on a four-wheeler to chase a rogue beast and hit a stump or a rock and end up in hospital. As our expert stockwoman Joni admitted, that's what happened to her early on in her career: she spent seven hours stuck under her buggy and almost lost her leg.

Neil's next reason is profitability. 'Once you get your livestock and your handling right, you can save fuel, you can save time,' he says. If your sheep don't run to the other end of the paddock whenever they hear a vehicle – 'deserting lambs, running their kilos off, filling themselves full of dust' – you're going to save time and money. It's the same with cattle.

If they're stressed they won't put on weight or their milk production will be lower. Using dogs rather than machinery can make all the difference. And the more meat on livestock at market, the better the profit margin for the producer.

Then there's animal welfare. 'When we learn to work livestock better and handle dogs to a greater level then our care for livestock is going to be up, and animal welfare is extremely important.'

Using dogs also enables greater care of the landscape and environment. Cell grazing allows farmers to frequently move livestock from one paddock to another, to give the land a chance to recover. 'So you're in the driver's seat of being able to control your pastures and the recovery of your plants and the prevention of soil erosion.' It's extremely rare to do this without a team of dogs to help shift the stock, as the average farmer doesn't have the people power required. The dogs also keep the animals calm, so the whole process is done with minimal impact on the livestock and the landscape.

And lastly there's the simple enjoyment that comes with working with settled animals. Neil has seen a T-shirt that reads: 'Sorry for what I said whilst working cattle.' Let's face it, you wouldn't want a swear jar in a yard. You'd all go broke. It's tough work and there are plenty of family squabbles. 'We have a lot of people leave our industry,' Neil says. 'A lot of sons and daughters don't stay home because of stuff like that.' Neil's convinced that by understanding dogs and livestock there'll be greater enjoyment in the industry, and the next generations will stay on the farm. He dreams of Australian farms remaining in Australian hands, with families running the show instead of overseas corporations.

If that all sounds ideal and you want a working dog to call your own, check your bank account. The record price for a kelpie was set in 2022 when Ross Gilmore paid $49,000 for a 20-month-old black and tan dog called Capree Eve.

It was about $20,000 more than the breeder, Chris Stapleton, was expecting, but as he told the ABC: 'I spent fifty years breeding this type of dog – she just didn't fall out of a tree, she's not an accident, she has been bred to do what she does.' The previous record was $35,200 and that was set just a year before for a kelpie named Hoover. Kelpies are hot property.

My curiosity got the better of me and I tracked Ross down late on a Sunday afternoon to ask him how he felt on that auction day as the price kept going up and the bids kept coming. I left a long message on his mobile explaining what I was hoping to ask him, but he could well have interpreted my question as, 'Are you bonkers?' He got back to me half an hour later and was happy to explain why he'd paid so much.

'Oh look, I went in pretty hard that day because you're not only buying a good dog but you're buying all of the breeding that's gone into her – and there were bloodlines going back so far that you knew exactly where she'd come from,' he told me. Ross and his brother help run a 2400-hectare sheep stud near Oberon on the New South Wales Central Tablelands. The family property was bought by their great-grandfather Alf, who'd emigrated from Ireland in the 1920s. He'd been working on the railway line through the Blue Mountains and when the crew arrived in the small outcrop of Black Springs, about 140 kilometres west of Sydney as the crow flies, Alf decided he'd buy land there because it reminded him of the lush fields of the home he'd left behind.

'I wish he hadn't,' Ross joked on the phone from the lambing shed where he'd been checking on pregnant ewes every hour and a half. 'It's cold and wet a lot of the year and about seven degrees at the moment and it's still only April.'

Ross told me things were going well with his very expensive kelpie purchase, but even with the pedigree breeding it was still a gamble. He wasn't sure if he'd be able to get Capree Eve to work as well as she had for her first handler, who'd had her since she was a pup. 'You don't know if you're going to click and if your personality is going to match. It took about six to eight weeks to settle her in properly. I spent a lot of one-on-one time building that relationship, but it's a fine line between being nice and friendly while reminding her you're the dominant figure.'

Ross has had between 15 and 20 good-quality working dogs over the years. He reckons one person working with two or three dogs is able to do what a team of two or three workers can do. 'That was one of the driving things, actually, about spending money on a dog with great potential, because it's becoming harder and harder to employ good labour. If you can substitute with a good dog, then it helps.' He said he'll definitely breed from Capree Eve, but he was still debating what mate to put her with.

Given Capree Eve's excellent bloodline, I'm thinking that's a decision you don't want to get wrong. But Neil McDonald tells his dog school students not to get too anxious about it all. 'There are people who sit there studying pedigrees and then there are others that just let two dogs mate,' he says. 'We need to be conscious of bloodlines, pedigrees, genetics and instinct but not be totally hung up by it.'

One of the challenges behind the scenes of season one was the haste with which the two highly respected breeders, Peter Barr and Joe Spicer, were asked to come up with a litter. Because of the timing of the show and the uncertainty of the ongoing impact of Covid, when the *Muster Dogs* production was finally green-lit, Peter and Joe were under the pump.

In the end, it was Joe Spicer's litter that had the numbers the producers required, but he hadn't been able to spend the time he normally would in preparing which dogs to mate and considering where they'd be going. The participants were all rapt to get a Joe Spicer dog, but it didn't necessarily mean that their dog would show the top-level genetics to warrant breeding from it.

These gorgeous border collies were waiting for me at Steve's home in Winton, Queensland. They weren't part of the official *Muster Dogs* litter but they'd grow up to become champion working dogs in their own right. (Ben Emery)

The *Muster Dogs* series-one participants and their dogs, at CJ's farm in the Northern Territory. L–R: CJ Scotney and Spice, Joni Hall and Chet, Rob Tuncks and Lucifer, Frank Finger and Annie, Aticia Grey and Gossip. (Steve Strike)

Ultrasounds on pregnant dogs can be useful but Debbie had so many pups wriggling inside her that the vets didn't know where one finished and another started. (Monica O'Brien)

Debbie laboured through the night inside Mick and Carolyn Hudson's kitchen near Dubbo, New South Wales. After fourteen hours Debbie had ten healthy pups. (Monica O'Brien)

Newborn pups' eyes don't open for two weeks. Carolyn checked their health each day by making sure their noses were moist. Indi stayed close to her mum until six weeks, when the pups were ready to wean. (Ben Emery)

Mick introduced the pups to stock early on to see if they had the instinct required to become good working dogs. Molly was raring to go. (Ben Emery)

The puppies spent their first four months together before heading to their new homes. (Carolyn Hudson)

Training started early at the Hudsons', even if Snow and the other pups thought they were simply having fun. (Melissa Spencer)

Molly sometimes struggled to let livestock know she was the boss. Russ Fowler in Tasmania spent a lot of time building her confidence. (Melissa Spencer)

Snow was all legs from the moment he was born but once he learned how to use them there was no stopping him. (Melissa Spencer)

Ash, who was named after tennis star Ash Barty, had a soft nature as a puppy and was keen to impress on the farm at Ban Ban Springs with her new family. (Melissa Spencer)

Indi started her training in the green fields near Dubbo but she quickly adapted to a hot, dry climate in northwest Queensland with Steve Elliott. (Melissa Spencer)

Buddy was the biggest pup of the litter and there wasn't much that intimidated him when he started working with his new trainer, Zoe Miller, in Katherine. (Ben Emery)

Carolyn has helped rear hundreds of puppies, but the *Muster Dogs* litter was extra special and saying goodbye was an emotional moment. (Ben Emery)

Frank Finger won hearts for taking on Lucifer (middle), who he renamed Luci, along with his winning dog, Annie (right). He then earned even more respect in series two by successfully training a deaf pup, Lucky (left). (Melissa Spencer)

Trainers Helen and Neil McDonald offered to help find participants for the first series. They had no idea they would end up being so pivotal to its success. (Monica O'Brien)

Neil is most comfortable in his beanie and tracksuit pants. He uses a rake as an extension of his arms to get the pups' attention during training sessions. (Richard Rowley)

Champion breeder, educator and trial dog champion Mick (with Ash) says you have to 'select the best, breed from the best and hope for the best'. (Melissa Spencer)

The finale shoot crew. Front row (L–R): Ben Emery, John Unwin, Melissa Spencer, Jonathan Jeffery, Sally Browning, Monica O'Brien, Michael Boughen. Back row (L–R): Jerry Batha, Bernie Kavanagh, Rich Rowley, Sid Tiney, Ash Eden, Aaron Kelly, Alison Huxley. (Jesse Smith)

Ben Emery, like the rest of the crew, studied the pups' training process so he could anticipate situations and make sure he captured their movements on camera. This also meant getting down for a dog's-eye view. (Monica O'Brien)

The crews would have one eye on the lens and hope the support team was keeping an eye on what was in front. (Melissa Spencer)

There were some peaceful moments for producer Monica O'Brien and cameraman Ben Emery, but filming puppies was often chaotic, noisy and a little messy. (Jesse Smith)

The livestock were generally unfazed by the noise, cameras and drones. But this one wanted to get a little closer to Monica on set in Clermont. (Jerry Batha)

A drone flies over participants Lily, Cilla, Steve, Zoe and Russ in the final days of filming. The crew used nine cameras, three drones and six GoPros to capture the finale from all angles. (Melissa Spencer)

When Buddy was small, Zoe would kneel so he could rest his paws on her outstretched arms. Eventually he grew big enough to reach her shoulders. (Simon Manzies)

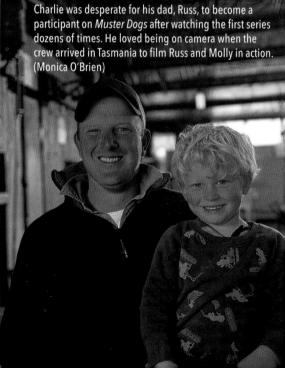

Charlie was desperate for his dad, Russ, to become a participant on *Muster Dogs* after watching the first series dozens of times. He loved being on camera when the crew arrived in Tasmania to film Russ and Molly in action. (Monica O'Brien)

Steve sometimes took different approaches to training Indi than those recommended by Neil, and his friend Keri was keen to learn as much as she could along the way. (Melissa Spencer)

Cilla compared training Ash to being on stage. You have to rehearse again and again if you want to deliver the best performance. (Monica O'Brien)

Lily juggled training Snow with her contract mustering jobs that would often take her hundreds of kilometres from her home in Wilcannia and last for weeks on end. (Sally Browning)

Mick Hudson gets help rounding up the sheep at his property. Experts believe one dog can do the work of three people on the farm. (Ben Emery)

Snow was a confident pup but there was an issue he could do nothing about: his colour. He had to convince the sheep he wasn't one of them and they had to respect him. (Melissa Spencer)

Cilla couldn't get Ash to make noise when she needed her to. So she packed up the kids and Ash and went to a dog school with series-one veteran Joni Hall. Joni made Ash so cranky she found her confidence to bark. (Jesse Smith)

Steve has a number of wheelchairs to use when training, including one that features just two wheels and looks like a Segway. When the dogs hear the noise of the wheels, they know it is time to get to work. (Brad Smith)

Molly trained mostly on sheep in Tasmania so would have to get used to mustering cattle for the finale. As she slides in the dirt of the yard to change direction, she doesn't take her eye off the stock. (Jesse Smith)

Zoe had battled through floods and drought, a sick dog and the end of a relationship. But on the final day of filming, as the sun set on series two, she and Buddy could hold their heads up high. (Jesse Smith)

CJ Scotney admitted she found her *Muster Dogs* pup, Spice, tricky to train and she's not sure if she'll breed from her. She had to dive into the research to try to understand why she couldn't get Spice to 'balance' as easily as her other dogs. Spice needed to be able to go to the tail of the mob and be happy to work there while CJ was at the front. But Spice didn't want to do that, instead only wanting to be either in the lead at the front or out to the side. Imagine if the lead beast was at 12pm; Spice would sit at 10am or 2pm – and need a lot of encouragement to leave that spot to work other parts of the mob.

Watching CJ try to wrangle Spice in some of the early episodes of series one made amateurs like me feel slightly better for not being able to get dogs off the couch let alone round up cattle. Spice was hard-headed about where she wanted to be and it meant that whenever CJ used Spice to muster she had to have a dog that complemented Spice on the opposite side. 'Spice is a team player but she's not one of my top dogs,' she says.

I know what it's like to go down a research rabbit hole. It was probably the moment when I was home alone in my apartment in Melbourne one Saturday evening, reading a University of Sydney research paper from 2015 on the 'Valuable Behavioural Phenotypes in Australian Farm Dogs' and making reassuring noises out loud to myself as I uncovered key facts, that I realised I'd gone deep into doggo world. It had crept up on me slowly, from those first inquiries from the *Muster Dogs* team to narrate the series to suddenly wanting to know every single bit of detail I could about Australia's legendary working dogs.

The level of genetic research being done was surprising to me, but it shouldn't have been. I know these dogs are worth money – an average price for a good working dog at the Rockhampton sales in 2022 was $7000 – so why wouldn't there be complex studies underway to keep improving the breeds? The researchers initially collected behavioural data for 4000 kelpies belonging to about 800 people in the livestock industry in a bid to nail down the science behind a good dog. By the end of the project, and leading up to the final report released in 2019, they had expanded it to nine different breeds and were looking at genetics. The kelpie and the collie made up the majority of the numbers, but the researchers also had a few of the following: the Australian cattle dog, koolie, black mouth cur, corgi, bearded collie, English shepherd and New Zealand huntaway.

Professor Claire Wade from the University of Sydney was a key member of the project. She grew up in the small country town of Bulahdelah, north of Sydney, and while she'd had dogs as a kid, she preferred her horses. One of her high-school projects was breeding budgerigars and she'd dreamed of studying animal genetics. She credits Scruffy and Jess, the two farm dogs who were her companions during her university work experience at Coolah near Dubbo, for really cementing her appreciation of the skill of working dogs. She then spent years in Boston learning from the very best genetic scientists: the international teams that sequenced, for the first time, the human genome. 'Gene-mapping is my real love,' she tells me from her home in Sydney. 'I really love it. I just love the puzzle of finding the genes that do things.'

So when Claire, now in her late fifties, talks about dogs and the research she and her fellow scientists have done, she's got the background and experience to back it up. They were able to highlight the super traits of working dogs – skill, instinct and fearlessness. The plan was to produce an unmatched DNA-based genomic resource for Australian working dog breeds that would allow dogs to be ranked like beef cattle and sheep. But it hasn't turned out as she'd anticipated.

'Well, we got some pushback from the breeders because so much of what they do is based on reputation. They didn't really want to be compared to each other on a scientific basis because they were worried it would do reputational harm,' she tells me.

She suggested another way for them to look at it: if genome profiles were published each year on the animals, breeders would be able to find the best dogs to match their own with. 'But the breeders said to me, "Well, we all know each other anyway," so that didn't convince them either.'

She doesn't sound frustrated when we're talking; rather she has a sense of appreciation for this tight-knit community, all of them experts in their own field. She has come to accept that the working dog world is less about genetics for the people at the core of it and more about relationships and trust.

The same could be said about the connection between a dog and its trainer. Without that relationship and trust, they will simply be animal and human. But with the right technical ingredients – breeding, genes, training, and so on – and a dash of synchronicity, they can become an inseparable pair, relying equally on each other as they prepare to tackle whatever task lies ahead.

And those tasks can prove challenging. Our series two *Muster Dogs* participants, Steve, Lily, Russ, Zoe and Cilla, not only had to make that connection, but then over nine months prove their dog had the skill to become a valuable workmate – and put their own abilities to the test at the same time.

CHAPTER 5

Training, Training, Training

Steve Elliott's home in Winton sits on the corner of a wide bitumen street, diagonally across from a sports field that, just a few weeks before the *Muster Dogs* film crew arrived, had been packed with crowds for the annual Way Out West festival. The 'Bulls! Bands! Bikes!' had moved on now and the only signs of life were a couple of workers pruning and mowing.

On the opposite side of the road is an old traditional Queenslander with not a shred of paint left on its wooden beams. The windows give the impression it's been years since they've been responsible for framing any glass. Steve told me someone in town bought it to use it for storage but there hadn't been a lot of movement.

A couple of four-wheel drives towing caravans cruised by. Winton only has a dozen or so streets, so I knew they'd find the highway north to Hughenden soon enough.

Steve's home, with its low stumps and tin roof, has a gently sloping ramp that wraps around it, with a 90-degree turn at the side of the house and another at the rear, which he hurtles down in his wheelchair. Near his shed, where he welds his cattle-branding irons, is a metal cage, about a metre and a half square, and lifted off the ground by four steel legs on wheels so it can be moved to follow the shade. Inside, seven pure-bred border collie puppies were finding their legs and their voices.

They scrabbled and scratched and fumbled to get their noses through the gaps to say hello, then went back to chewing at a solid block of frozen raw mince, which disappeared into their bellies before it had time to thaw in the heat. Two were girls, the other five were boys, and they were born just shy of two months before we arrived to film Steve and his friend Keri and their dogs.

'Surprise!' *Muster Dogs* filmmaker Monica O'Brien called out as I walked up the dirt driveway and saw the pups for the first time. It's funny to think that despite being so closely attached to series one of *Muster Dogs*, I didn't actually spend any time with the dogs. Viewers often assumed I had the best job in the world because it involved playing with puppies but, as the narrator, I did all my work in an audio booth after the filming had already happened.

Monica, on the other hand, had managed a lot of time with the dogs on series one, despite the Covid border challenges. She doesn't have a dog back in the Sydney apartment she shares with her family. Brad says he worries a pet would be either suffocated with love and attention when everyone is home or spend its days thinking, *Hey, where has everyone gone?* when the family is at work and school.

Monica was hoping it would be a nice surprise for me to discover puppies at Steve's place and it was. They'd been a bit of a surprise even to Steve, who'd bought a dog called Freckle from Mitch Perez, a breeder down south, not expecting her to be pregnant by the time she arrived in Winton.

'We'd put Huey over Lottie to get Kenny, and then Mitch had Freckle and asked if I wanted Freckle,' Steve said, rattling through a sample of the complex relationships of the working dog world. 'And then Freckle was on heat before he got her up here so he put Kenny over Freckle and that's how the dog came to me in pup.'

I nodded, pretending I could sketch out the family tree from his quick-fire genealogy details.

Most pure-bred working dogs have a prefix indicating the registered kennel name that is unique to each breeder. It's a bit like naming the make of a car and then the model. For example, Mitch Perez's dogs will have 'MDP' as the prefix.

Freckle's full name is Clancy's Creek Freckle. Steve's dogs have 'Diamantina' as the prefix because that's how he's registered. Joe Spicer in Hamilton, Victoria, has 'GoGetta' as a prefix, so *Muster Dogs* winner Annie is actually GoGetta Annie. For the sake of the show, we kept things simple by just calling the dogs by the names their new owners gave them. In series one our dogs were Lucifer (Rob), Chet (Joni), Spice (CJ), Gossip (Aticia) and Annie (Frank). In series two we had Buddy (Zoe), Ash (Cilla), Indi (Steve), Molly (Russ) and Snow (Lily).

The new puppies at Steve's place were still nameless, but he's got an old fridge close to his welding bench that offers some possibilities. The fridge is the kind that often ends up in garages and backyard sheds, destined to hold a few slabs of beer and maybe the leftovers of a big family lunch once a year. It's covered in red dust, but you can make out the names Steve has contemplated over the years, written in thick black ink: Punter, Persie, Stinky, Fidget. There are dozens of them on the once-white door, some of them crossed out after they've been used.

For the pups' first few months of life, Steve would do little more than feed, exercise and bond with them. Once they hit the three-month mark, he would start training them and watch for the traits he likes to see: a calm mind, a good work ethic, and what he calls 'cover' – being able to keep control of a small mob of livestock. Then he would decide which ones he liked best and sell the others at auction when they were around a year old. He could get up to $8000 for each pup, if they had the working instinct.

'We can't keep them all, you know, Lisa,' he said as Keri unlocked the cage and he watched the pups gingerly tap their paws on the plank of wood she'd propped there as a slide. 'And, besides, it will give someone else the chance to own a good working dog.'

The pups weren't used to the outside world, and they clung to the security of their cage until they got a push and a shove from one of their siblings. When they finally took the plunge and hit the ground they scooted to every corner of the yard. Ben Emery, the camera operator on this shoot, was making a valiant effort to try to keep them in his viewfinder but they were throwing themselves into the wet grass and discovering puddles in holes where the sprinkler had sprayed water, then racing off for a wrestle, nipping each other with the excitement of freedom.

'The puppies are incredibly difficult to film,' Ben told me later, stating the obvious. 'Monica and Brad would like things shot from the dog perspective, so that's down low, but as soon as you get down low, the puppies are climbing all over you. Their noses are right up against the lens; they're licking it, they're licking you.'

I was starting to think *Muster Dogs* might have been why Ben's long hair, tied in a knot under his baseball cap, was showing signs of grey. The rest of us were having fun watching those bundles perform on the lawn, but Ben and sound recordist Ash Eden were a picture of concentration.

Ben filmed a few sequences for series one but had been responsible for a lot of the work in series two. 'As a newbie, the first time I was chasing dogs it was impossible, but once they're up and trained and once you understand what it is they do and what the handlers are asking of them they're kind of predictable and you start to learn it too.'

He avoided catastrophe that day in Winton, although his tripod did have a close encounter with a puppy with diarrhoea; nothing that a drenching in antiseptic couldn't fix. 'It was cute but also kind of gross,' he said.

You're never far from poo on a farm. Dried cow patties are safe territory. Landing on them can help you avoid the prickles in the grass when you're barefoot. But stepping in wet dung is a sensation you never want repeated.

Ben's experience of learning to film animals reminded me of a time when I was living and working in the United States. Australia was in the middle of long negotiations over a free trade agreement, and the ABC's international editor wanted me to investigate how a free trade deal with the US had affected other countries. So just as negotiations were reaching their end point I decided to head to Canada, which had been part of a free trade zone (NAFTA) with the US and Mexico since 1994. Off I flew to Ottawa with Dan, the camera operator. It was winter and brutally cold. We picked up a rental car and arranged to meet a farmer at his dairy early the next morning.

It was still dark outside when we left the motel and headed north, past what seemed like endless snowbanks. As we turned into the farm, I could see steam escaping through the vents of the barn. Like most dairy farmers, the family we interviewed that morning were intent on making sure their cows were comfortable. The milking area was insulated, trapping the warmth generated by the cows. The workers would often give the cows a rub on the back as they walked past to check the robotic milkers were working properly. The music being played through the speakers had to be not too loud, not too soft, but like the three bears and their porridge, just right. All of that could affect the quality of the milk and the farm's bottom line.

I had the easier task of chatting to the farmers while Dan wrangled the camera and tripod, fiddling with the lens focus and the sound, and making sure he didn't 'double button' – that is, accidentally hit the record button twice with frozen fingers and discover too late that he'd recorded absolutely nothing. As usual, he was completely focused on the task at hand, which was why he didn't notice the slight lift of the cow's tail as it prepared to empty its bowels. A quick shout and he stepped back just in time to miss the manure splashing down.

We laughed about it later and I told him about all the near misses that had been part of Millar family folklore, stories retold with glee whenever my family got together. My older siblings knew what it meant when the pastures were green in Kilkivan: the dung would be runny and trying to catch it on a shovel in the shed was damn near impossible. My siblings had all done their fair share of milking cows in the pre-dawn light and remembered only too well the moment when a cow with dung on its tail went to flick a pesky fly and the poor milker ended up with dung on their face.

I've always thought the decade I spent overseas, based in Washington and London for the ABC, was a privilege, a dream come true for a country kid who always wanted to be a journalist. But it would be naïve to think it didn't leave a mark. You can't witness countless terrorist attacks, school shootings, earthquakes and fires without being affected in some way.

One night over a beer in Winton, Ben and I got talking about the career paths that led us to *Muster Dogs*. Ben grew up in the small coastal hamlet of Haslam in South Australia. About 35 people called it home, and his parents owned the general store, frequented by the fishermen and interstate truckers who'd pass through. His friends from school came from properties but that was the closest he came to being on the land. He left for Canberra in Grade Nine to finish his schooling and, with an English teacher's encouragement, began studying advertising and media.

His career path was similar to a lot of ambitious camera operators: side hustles of weekend wedding videos and weekday regional news and then the break into a metropolitan newsroom. From there, he headed overseas at the urging of a friend who'd joined the newly created Al Jazeera English channel in the mid 2000s. Back then, the original Doha-based Arabic-language network was still viewed with suspicion as a mouthpiece for the Taliban in the years after the September 11 attacks, a period I had covered as a reporter in Washington DC.

Ben had spent more than a decade working for Al Jazeera around the world, never far from the big stories. He was on the ground for the London bombings in 2005, the war in Afghanistan and, one of the hardest he covered, Typhoon Haiyan that ripped through Southeast Asia in 2013. 'We choppered in and filmed for five days, living in amongst it, bodies lying around everywhere, rotting,' he recalled.

We'd never met before the Winton trip, but when we started talking about our different assignments, we realised we'd both been in Bali in 2005 for the trial of Australian Schapelle Corby, who was sentenced to 20 years for importing cannabis. Ben was working for Channel 7 and I was at the ABC. The media attention had been intense. Hundreds of people were there to witness the final verdict, so it's no surprise our paths hadn't crossed. But Ben and I both remember the weirdness of it all – the courtroom in what felt like a small classroom, seemingly hundreds of cameras crushed up against the windows and the one squat toilet that quickly filled to capacity early in the day.

Ben Emery, director of photography on series two. (Monica O'Brien)

Molly staring down livestock. (Brad Smith)

'Gawd,' I said to him, screwing up my nose at the memory. 'Look at us now – playing with puppies and stepping in dog poo!'

'Yeah, to be honest, I felt super lucky I got to travel,' he replied, as the solo singer belting out covers at the pub threatened to drown us out. 'There are very few countries I haven't been to in the world, but I was burnt out. I'd rather be doing this, and to be able to do it with good people makes it even better.'

I asked him if he thought filming series two of *Muster Dogs* felt different to working on the first one. 'I reckon because of the success of the first series, this time round people feel like maybe they have more to lose if they don't do well. We are spending a lot of time with people when they are going through big moments of stress in front of the cameras.'

Most of our participants had long histories working with dogs. But having a camera trained on them as they completed the milestone tasks for each episode could make even the most experienced handler feel a little uncomfortable.

*

Before I go any further, let me explain a few of the terms that might pop up in this chapter on training. You'll be able to relate to some of them whether you have a working dog or a couch potato.

Balance: the position of a dog in relation to the handler. If the handler is at six o'clock then the dog will be sent to twelve o'clock to gather up the stock. The dog should then only work between the arc of nine o'clock and three o'clock.

Cast: the dog's ability to run in a wide arc around the mob. We don't want to unfairly pick on Rob's dog Lucifer but he had a habit early on of just running straight at the stock, which didn't really work for anyone – Lucifer, Rob or the sheep! What handlers are looking for is a cast that is a bit like the shape of a pear, where the dogs go out wide at the bottom but then come back in near the head of the mob.

Cover: the dog's ability to keep the mob together by covering any possible escape.

Driving: how the dog moves the stock away from the handler in a given direction.

Drawing: how the dog moves the stock towards the handler.

Flight zone: the distance the dog can approach before the stock moves. The flight zone is dynamic, and its size and shape depend on several factors, including breed, age, disposition, temperament, past handling, the dog's approach and their psychological and physical state.

Gather: how the dog brings stock from a scattered position into a group.

Eye: the dog's ability to stare down an animal many times its size. The dog will 'stalk' the stock with their head lowered in a predatory stance, staring intently. For example, Keri noticed very early on in series two that her dog Bobby McGee had a strong presence. He was intense and the animals could sense this dog was powerful. You'll often see these dogs approach animals in a low crawl. But Bobby McGee was still a young dog and Keri knew he didn't have the confidence to back up his 'eye', so he was at risk of getting hurt without more training.

Herding instinct: the dog's natural desire to work stock.

Lift: the initial push the dog uses to move stock.

Pressure point: the exact position and distance the dog needs to be from the stock to get them moving efficiently.

Sticky: a dog's ability to show eye so intently on the stock that it appears to be mesmerised and frozen.

Force: the dog's ability to get livestock moving if they look like they're going to be stragglers.

Temperament: this is just what you expect; the handlers are looking for a desire in the dog to please its master. You'll see some of our participants talking about their dogs just 'wanting to get to work' and showing they're ready to accept a command and make their owners happy.

Bark and bite: you may need both of these in a dog, but as a handler you want to be the one who can control it. At the wrong time and with the incorrect level of strength or effort, it can be bad news for the livestock. Your dog should only be barking when you want them to bark.

Backing: you'll have seen this in photos plenty of times – it's the incredibly graceful leaping of a working dog from the back of one sheep to another. It's a signature move that probably makes the rest of the dog world wonder if collies and kelpies might be a bit of a show-off at their core. 'Backing' does the job, though – it gets the dog from one end of a logjam to the other in the quickest way possible.

*

There's no doubt that dogs can show an instinct very early on. Our participants and trainers talk about when they're going to 'start' a dog. Being able to check if a puppy has the instinct and is likely to be a good worker is important because you don't want to spend years training a dog that isn't interested in the job.

Ben Emery remembers seeing breeder Mick Hudson putting the three-month-old *Muster Dogs* puppies in front of stock for the very first time. 'Their first experience – and they go straight into stalking mode, down low, around to the head of the mob,' he said. 'It was extraordinary to watch them do something they'd never been taught to do, such a skill.'

So what process is involved in taking a newly born pup to a fully fledged, trained working dog? There are many different techniques for how to initially handle litters and none are particularly right or wrong.

Rob Tuncks says he's had pups as young as six weeks old out working livestock. And he's also had puppies like his dog Max, who was a bit slower off the mark. Max spent the first year of his life showing no inclination to work. Some farmers would have chosen not to keep a dog like Max, but Rob had no choice because his partner had fallen in love with him. 'So he got to hang around,' Rob says, 'and then he started working when he was twelve months old and ended up quite a good dog!'

Joe Spicer started removing the kelpie pups for series one from their mum, Truce, when they were four or five weeks old, putting them in an area where they could run around.

'The pups can go free range and it lets us learn a lot more about them, the characters, and the individual natures,' he says. They'll jump over logs and through fences during this period, and because Joe knew a little about the prospective participants on the show, he started thinking about each dog's nature, and what type of work they would suit. 'Quite often there's a correlation between a more outgoing puppy and a pushier dog or a more forceful dog.'

Joe knew that Frank, CJ, Joni, Rob and Aticia all had different personalities: some of them were quieter and would want their dogs to be working their stock slowly and calmly. 'So I took that into account as I watched the puppies early on. They're just roly-poly playing in the paddock and I've put some sheep in there and I watch their reaction to the sheep.'

Even at that young age, they started showing a bit of instinct as Joe sat on a drum and quietly observed them. How they ate was also revealing. Some came up to him for food while others hung off his pants or sat back and waited. And he watched how they interacted with each other. He started to see a shift as the pups matured. The runt that he thought was going to be outgoing became more reserved, something that often happens. He decided to keep that one for himself and named it Trunk. None of the other participants knew that their *Muster Dogs* pups had another sibling until they gathered in the Northern Territory for the final days of filming and Joe surprised them by bringing along Trunk.

Mick Hudson says the runt always needs a bit more attention. 'There's a runt generally in a larger litter because the bigger pups push the little pup off the teat and he gets weaker and weaker, and often he'll die. We'll try to save it by making sure the bigger pups are put in the basket and the little pup gets a good drink from the mum before they go back on supplement feed.'

Carolyn Hudson started handling the border collie pups in series two as soon as they were born, but just for brief moments, picking them up once a day. She watched them closely to make sure their noses stayed moist; if their noses were to go dry, she'd be worried they were sick. She dipped their little faces in soft food, maybe some canned food, and added a little warm milk. 'By the time they're four weeks, she'll have them eating and drinking – and ready to wean at six weeks,' Mick says. If it's a bigger litter, like our pups in series two, then they wean them earlier, depending on how the mother is handling things.

Carolyn says once they're weaned you get to know the personalities, especially if one is more tentative than the others. She wasn't supposed to name the about-to-be famous pups while she cared for them for those first few months – that honour was for the participants – but she couldn't resist. The names didn't stick because our participants chose different monikers for them, but it helped her while she had them.

'Especially if one's been a bit naughty or something, I need to have a name so it will recognise it's getting into trouble,' she told me, wondering if she should be revealing this secret. 'And besides, when I say "Puppy, puppy, puppy," you'll end up with all of them running towards you. Sometimes Mick will change the name of a dog. We had one I called Cindy and he changed it to Girl because he was trying to get her to come to him and he kept on saying, "Good girl, good girl" and so he said, "OK, she's called Girl now."'

Carolyn had a soft spot for the completely white one, who she quickly realised was deaf. The other pups would be awake and scrabbling around in the cage and he would be sound asleep. She admits to losing him twice when she was giving them all a run because he lost sight of them and couldn't hear her voice as he was off investigating his surroundings. But she thinks his other senses must be heightened. The first time he got lost, he followed the main track back to the property. The second time, though, they were in a different paddock, and the pups had followed Carolyn as she rode the motorbike to the furthest point near a dam. 'He was gone,' she told me. 'I couldn't see him anywhere. But you know what he did? He pelted for home, exactly the way he came because he must have been able to smell where we'd come from – and, sure enough, he was in the pen waiting for me when I got back to the house.'

Carolyn's strong connection to the pups was revealed in an emotional moment early on in series two when she had to say goodbye. With Mick away a lot, she'd often been the only human contact for the puppies. No wonder she felt protective of them all.

The process of writing this book and being able to delve

into people's lives has given me an insight into their stoic natures. Carolyn strikes me as a woman who has spent her life competently dealing with whatever situation she's forced to confront. Her own pregnancy is just one example. She was expecting twins when she and Mick were living on the sheep, cattle and goat property he'd bought in western New South Wales. Cobar was their closest town, about 110 kilometres away, and Carolyn was doing casual work at the pub there, as well as at a freight company in town, to keep money coming in during a terrible drought. The obstetrician would come to town every so often, but two months before her due date Carolyn was rushed to Dubbo hospital, even further from home.

'I told the doctor I felt fine, but my blood pressure was extremely high and I ended up there for three weeks, and the boys were then born six weeks premmie,' she told me, explaining the added difficulties of this high-risk pregnancy in the outback. 'And then we had three trips to Sydney with the boys in those first days. Harry got flown out the day after he was born because he had trouble breathing and then he was brought back in a week and his brother, Ben, and I had to be flown to Sydney for medical help.'

They were in the middle of the raging drought we now know as the Millennium Drought. In some parts of Australia it would last until 2009. 'Poor Mick was pulling sheep and goats out of bogged dams. It was a nightmare time.' Mick would cut branches off the mulga scrub for the animals, as stock feed was scarce. They took on huge debts, freighting food in and selling animals at a loss. Mick was working 12 hours a day on the property to try to keep their herds alive. 'We had to try to get some money in the bank because the bills don't stop just because your wife's in hospital,' Carolyn said. 'That's the farmer's life; you take the good with the bad.'

When she got home with the babies, she and Mick would drive across their huge paddocks, opening and shutting dozens of gates, feeding grain to the sheep out of a cart. 'We had to do it that way because if we fed them at the gate in the first paddock, they'd just stay there and not go out to try to forage. And then the eagles would swoop in and take the lambs.'

When the boys were toddlers, Carolyn would drive long distances to other properties to join a travelling playgroup: a couple of young women and their mobile van, providing toys and entertainment for the bush kids. And then a year or so later she'd drive one hour each way to take them to preschool once a fortnight. 'I'd spend the day in town after dropping them off, and do the shopping or pay the bills and then pick them up at the end of the day and we'd come home again.' That was what you did in the bush, she said, if you wanted your children to know what it was like to have other kids and not just adults for company.

So when Carolyn cried in the opening scenes of the first episode of series two, saying goodbye to the gorgeous border collies she'd cared for, it was both out of character and completely natural.

At least she knew they were going to wonderful homes. Our *Muster Dogs* participants had already received their list of milestone targets for the months ahead and arrangements were made for the camera crew to return to check in on their progress. They also got some early tips from trainer Neil McDonald, including a video starting with the basics – how to pick up a pup. Neil told them a good dog trainer is someone who understands how dogs work and how livestock acts.

'They also have to be firm but fair leaders, develop comradeship and a sense of humour with the dog, and the dog has to know it's special to them. If they have all that, then they will have success,' Neil says in the video. Imagine it's the end of a long day, he says, when tempers have gone up along with the temperature and things aren't going the right way, but your dog still wants to stick with you. It's that good relationship that counts.

Our kelpies in series one stayed with breeder Joe Spicer until they were three months old and they were tested on their set targets at four, six, nine and twelve months old. The milestones for our border collies in series two were slightly different. They stayed with Carolyn and Mick until they were almost four months old and were tested on their targets at five, seven and ten months old. Mick and Carolyn wanted to make sure the collie puppies were showing some early instinct on stock and had safely come through their vaccinations. Their final milestone test was held, just like for series one, when they were a year old.

'All dogs are different,' Neil told me when I caught up with him on the phone. He was in Wudinna on the Eyre Peninsula in South Australia, and even though it was only 8.30 on a Sunday morning he'd already driven 300 kilometres and had another 800 to go to get home to his property in Keith that day. His work as a dog trainer was now keeping him on the road for nine months of the year.

'Mick wanted to make sure the dogs had started working with livestock before he handed them over and quite often it's viewed that the collies are a little slower to get there.' But Neil was quick to make sure he wasn't escalating a 'collies versus kelpies' debate. 'We're doing them an injustice if we start comparing like Ford versus Holden. It's the family lines within the breed that are telling.'

All ten participants from both series were asked to keep their appearance in *Muster Dogs* a secret, even from their extended families. That was simply too hard for some of them, especially those living in small country towns. Nevertheless, they had to try to find a way to train their new Muster Dog away from prying eyes. Neil would check in with them at each milestone, and decisions would be made about whether the pups were given a fail or a pass. 'I really don't see it as a television series,' he said about the process. 'It's just me giving advice to someone with a dog.' But he was conscious of not wanting to leave anyone exposed. The participants were allowed to call him and Helen at any time to ask for advice.

The whole concept of *Muster Dogs*, after all, was an experiment. The participants had been told not to worry if they felt their dog wasn't able to accomplish any given milestone. The dog might have been unwell, or the property might have been destocked. The participants had different work schedules and environmental issues, and it might have ended up being stressful if the producers hadn't insisted the point was for them to enjoy the experience.

The first email they received from the show's makers said: 'That's why we're observing the entire period, as the dogs will have different strengths at different times and seeing those similarities and variations will be really interesting for our audience and also help people get a better understanding of a work cycle for you and also how helpful and valuable these dogs are to your lives and business. We're not looking for perfection.'

Each of the participants was asked to prepare for the tasks ahead by getting a trainer mob in place. This is a small group of animals, generally either sheep or cattle, that have already been educated to behave well around other stock and to move calmly. The participants were warned that getting to stage one (the five-month milestones) would be a busy time.

By the time the pups were five months old, the participants were told the pups needed to respect them and have bonded with them. They were sent emails with the list of tasks to meet at each milestone. This was the first stage:

- We want to see a happy fresh-faced pup that demonstrates the correct timing of patting and rewarding whilst looking at you.
- You should be able to verbally communicate with the dog and have the dog communicate back with the tilt of the head or the prick of the ears. To show the connection that has been developed – your 'bluetooth' with that dog.
- The pup will need to drag a 3-metre-length rope and not be distracted by the rope.
- To catch a pup, have an encouraging noise or call its name and be in position to step on the rope to enforce the call.
- The pup needs to be relaxed when picked up and patted on the tummy without turning into a squid.
- You should be able to walk it on a loose lead.
- You should be able to distract it from licking other dogs' faces by flicking the rope, stamping the feet or using a gruff voice tone.
- The pup should be able to feed with older dogs – and not to roll or stand in the food.
- The pup should be good manners and be calm on the back of the ute or short chain.

The participants were also told it would be good to see some instinct in the pup, to see whether it had an urge to stalk and chase the trainer mob.

The next milestone note started with these encouraging words: 'If you survive this yappy puppy time, stage two should be a bit smoother.'

When the pups were seven months old, the participants were told:

- The collies should be well socialised with other dogs and have the fundamentals to stop and sit and to show a strong working instinct.
- They should walk beside you on a loose lead or no lead at all.
- They should be comfortable to jump on a hay bale or motorbike.
- Providing the pup has good instincts, it should have started basic herding.

The pups were expected to be able to perform a 'quarter bubble' on educated livestock, which means that they should be able to keep a group of livestock in a corner of the yard, with fences on two sides to help them. Later on they'd need to perform a 'half bubble', which is to hold a group of livestock in one spot along a straight fence line, with no corners to help keep the stock in place; and then eventually a 'full bubble', where the livestock would be in the middle of the yard with the dog controlling them from all sides, with no fences at all to help.

When the pups were ten months old, they'd be tested on the stage three milestones.

- By now a good working pup will be showing respect to you and the pack and know its place in the pack.
- The pup should know not to get on a bike without being told.
- You should be able to sit on a couch or chair with the dog remaining in sitting or standing position beside you when someone, or another dog, enters the room or yards.
- The dog should be able to come around the side of the mob and bring stock to you. It should be gaining more skills and showing real interest and desire to work.
- The dog should be able to do a basic cast – maybe 30 metres.

Their stage four note (the one-year milestones) began with this frank insight: 'You've either nailed it by now or you're battling to rein in the pup. Your pup should be comfortable and useful in the pack. It should be showing a hunger to improve but not overstep its position. Your pup should fit into the pack without mucking up and interfering with what the other dogs are doing.'

At this point, the collie pups would now be young dogs and would be expected to do the following:

- Bring a small mob of livestock to you.
- Demonstrate a good sit or stop.
- Come to the handler when called with one or two requests at most.
- Be able to walk into a yard with stock but not work the stock unless told to.
- Immediately respond to being called off stock when the handler calls.
- Work in a team with other dogs to block up a reasonable mob of stock.
- Sit patiently but alert outside the yard waiting to block up stock.

It all sounds doable, especially because our participants were starting with some experience. But some had been training dogs for longer than others. Steve was so experienced that when the *Muster Dogs* producers rang him, his friend Keri wondered if they were going to get *him* to train the participants. At the other end of the scale, Cilla had bucketloads of enthusiasm and plenty of years on the land but had never really dedicated herself to dog training. They were all open to Neil's thoughts, though – something, he said, that doesn't always happen at the dog schools he's conducted.

'Sometimes the person down the front is smiling at me but goes home and they never implement any of this – and there's someone down the back with a little bit of a frown and a grumble and they go home and really kick goals,' he said. 'Social media lets us see a little bit more of how people go when they get home. They reprogram their dogs, they reprogram their livestock, and some might even change their yard design. That's where I get my jollies, to see something that people have learned that they've been able to benefit from.'

A television audience that had never witnessed dogs being trained was sometimes baffled by what was on screen in series one. Neil would put his arm out as if to point at one of the livestock and the dog would run in the opposite direction. 'But you're not actually pointing,' he told me. 'You're blocking the dog from coming around, so when he sees your arm he knows he can't get through there so he heads away from where you're blocking.'

It's why Neil uses a rake. He says it's a good visual for the dog, making his arm look much longer than it is. By swinging the rake out, he leaves the dogs in no doubt they have to go the opposite way.

'A natural instinct of a dog is to bring back livestock, while the natural instinct of livestock is to get away,' he said, explaining the basis of the duel between the dogs and the livestock. 'So obviously there's going to be a little bit of a squabble until that gets sorted out. Eventually if the dog's working well, the livestock surrender from escaping and come back to the person controlling the dog, and then the livestock get relief being with that person so that's what changes the psyche of the mob.'

A good dog will put pressure on livestock but know when to release and give them relief from that pressure. Rob Tuncks told me what he wants to see in his dog: 'It's got to have enough presence that if the animal turns on the dog, the dog can give it a whack on the nose, but it's not allowed to bite their heel. The dog's got to be one hundred per cent respectful of the livestock. If the livestock's doing the right thing, the dog has to leave it alone and not cause trouble because, as soon as the dog starts to squabble, the livestock will turn around and have a fight with the dog and then everything gets out of control.'

Neil's been running dog schools for 34 years. Before that he had a string of jobs off the farm to bring in more money, like mulesing sheep (a now controversial method of cutting skin from around an animal's buttocks to prevent flystrike in the wool and infections). So many people I've spoken to have talked about their 'off-farm' jobs. The reality is that many properties simply can't support the families who live there. Three decades after setting up his own dog school, Neil can't count the number of dogs and trainers he's helped – easily in the thousands. While the techniques have been refined over the years, there are some truths that have never changed.

'I actually don't think there's such a thing as a dog trainer,' Neil explained as he laid out his approach to me. 'You're a situation creator. You create a situation where the dog does something because of natural instinct, and you immediately label the action the dog is about to take.'

For instance, if a dog goes to the right of the mob, Neil suggests you have a term to tell the dog what they're doing. It might be 'Go to the right' or 'Go anti-clockwise'. When a dog is about to sit, you say 'Sit' just before they do it. You're labelling that action for them so they can start to understand commands. 'Normally, for a lot of people, when a dog rushes in and puts too much pressure on the livestock, they say, "Steady, steady." The dog's actually hearing the command "Steady" when it's forcing too hard.' It's counterproductive, Neil explained, and doesn't help the dog or the handler.

It doesn't matter what words you use or how many you have; by saying them out loud and with the right tone just as a dog is doing that action, you'll start the process of labelling. The dog will then equate that word with that action. In a short amount of time you'll be saying 'Sit' and the dog will obey your command and sit.

Over the years that Joni Hall has moved from one contracting job to another in Western Australia and the Northern Territory, she has tried to follow Neil's philosophy with her 20 or so dogs. 'It's the five Rs,' she told me. 'It's request, reinforce, response, release, reward.' Although it doesn't always go that way for the determined cattlewoman. With some dogs, it's 'request, remind, remind, remind, remind, reinforce, get a pat'. And sometimes it's just reinforce, she says, depending on how much sleep she's had the night before.

Despite all the training he's done, Neil never tires of the adventure of starting with a fresh group, especially for the two *Muster Dogs* series. And despite knowing quite a few of the selected team, he was never sure how it was going to go. 'People are so passionate, and they know there's a bit at stake here. A lot of people get dogs and it's like getting a pup at Christmas – by New Year's Day sometimes the fun factor is gone. But not with these *Muster Dogs* participants. They know all eyes are on them. I imagine these dogs are having more effort put into them than any other dog they've had in their life.'

Neil's top advice for the participants was to make sure they were able to tie the dog up or have it in a cage when they weren't around. But seeing dogs in cages proved confronting for many city dog owners, who watched the first series of *Muster Dogs* and couldn't imagine ever putting their own dogs in one.

When I was a kid, my best friend, Robynne, lived on a farm 30 minutes out of Kilkivan, and the dogs on her family's property all had their own separate kennels away from the house, keeping them safe from wild weather. This was the 1970s and the kennels were made from hollowed-out logs with a bit of corrugated roof sheeting to stop the water seeping through.

Cages on farms these days tend to be made of metal, abutting each other, with wire fencing on at least one side facing out. Each dog normally has its own cage and it can appear pretty stark to someone not from the land. There isn't any bedding – they'd likely rip it up, or it would get wet and mouldy or very smelly.

I challenged all our trainers and breeders on the issue of cages and pushed them about the seemingly harsh approach, but they were adamant it's for the dog's own safety. 'If you don't keep them caged, the dog's mind can go floaty, and it can go anywhere,' Neil said. 'It's trained to work and it will race off in search of stock to work on, and the risk of it being run over is high. Keeping them alive is my number-one advice.'

Rob is a firm believer in cages too. 'People think they want to see the dogs be free and running around. Well, in the city they're locked in cages too, just slightly bigger ones called backyards. My dogs have got their cages and they're under trees and they're sheltered, and they've got water on tap.' Like the other participants, Rob keeps each dog in a separate cage. 'You can't have them all together because they'll form a pack and they'll start picking on one of the dogs – or when you take them out working, they'll work for themselves and they won't work for you. But the most important thing is it keeps them safe, and they won't end up under a wheel or just going off madly looking for something to round up.'

There's nothing more upsetting to Neil than seeing unrestrained dogs on the backs of utes. I hated confessing to him that I remember family friends from 50 years ago who would drive along with their dog on top of the hay truck and keep an eye on it by watching its shadow. If the shadow disappeared, they'd come to a screeching halt to check the dog was still on top. But times have changed, and most people are more conscious of doing the right thing. Still, Neil is alarmed at how many people don't.

'What disappoints me the most is the age-old thing of getting people to tie dogs up when they're not using them and learn to put them on the back of a ute in a way where they can't hang, tangle, choke or fall off,' he said. 'I explain this with great detail at a school – it probably takes me an hour – and then people will say goodbye and drive away with their dogs loose on the back of the ute or tied on a rope that they can chew through, or they've got cage doors that can spring open, and the list goes on.'

You don't have to hang out with Neil for long to see just how much he cares for these animals. So much, in fact, that he couldn't pick a favourite out of our *Muster Dogs* pups. He was hoping they'd all pass every milestone so that when they got to the final it would be a dead heat. And if there had to be a winner, he was hoping it would be because of something unpredictable, like a gate blowing shut or a branch snapping on a tree and spooking the sheep. 'I'd like all their accomplishments to be appreciated,' he said.

But that wasn't the aim of the game. It was a friendly competition – but a competition nonetheless. There was always going to be one Muster Dog who was considered the champion at the end of the series – with a bit of stress, a lot of fun and more than a few missteps along the way. In series one, it was Frank's dog, Annie. So who would it be in series two?

CHAPTER 6

Technical Talk

One chilly Sunday morning, as heavy rain clouds tracked over this southeastern corner of South Australia, Neil and Helen McDonald sat at their dining room table, staring intently at their laptop. Helen's baseball caps were hooked on the joints of a native pine post helping support the ceiling in the middle of the room. A pair of jeans and a checked farm shirt had been flung over a clotheshorse near the fireplace, and Helen apologised for the dust under the chairs.

This is home, the same one that Neil grew up in, although it's unrecognisable from the original basic abode of his boyhood. The couple don't spend a lot of time here at the house. It's the shed, a few hundred metres away, that is at the centre of their farm and dog work.

I was there with them to watch footage of the series-two participants' attempts to pass their ten-month milestones. I'd been trying to connect to the wifi so we could project the laptop screen onto their large television, but I failed at the first technical hurdle, and we laughed that I hadn't found the 'bluetooth'. This word that Neil uses to describe the bond between a dog and its master became one of several catchphrases from series one. With producer Monica taking notes, Helen and Neil got down to business on the smaller laptop screen.

Australia is a big country, but the working dog world is small. While some participants joined *Muster Dogs* after answering social media call-outs, it was Neil who encouraged others to sign up, after seeing them in action at his schools. But he never imagined he and Helen would become so central to the program, appearing in both series and becoming touchstones for those taking part.

'Hang on, can I see that again?' he piped up when we saw footage of Russ Fowler sending his dog, Molly, to round up sheep. It was the '30-metre cast' test. The farmer has to send the dog on its mission 30 metres away from the mob. We watched as Molly tried to round them up, but one sheep headed straight for her instead of giving ground, seemingly determined to prove it was the boss. 'Oh jeez, that's an aggressive sheep in there,' Helen observed.

Neil wasn't impressed. He threw his hands up to his head as he witnessed another misdemeanour. 'Can we give the dog a pass and Russ a fail? Why the hell did he keep that one sheep in that mob?' Monica agreed, and Russ and Molly got half a point.

They kept going, passing comments while watching the footage, as Monica hit play, pause and rewind. Neil did an exaggerated eye roll when he heard Cilla, on her property in Ban Ban Springs, effusively praise her dog, Ash, with a 'Good doggy, you goooood doggy.' He gives the impression he doesn't have a sentimental side, but I spied a smile and could see he was actually enjoying the process. Because the judges were not onsite when these challenges were being performed, the participants didn't know how they were being assessed at each one. They did get feedback, but it would be eight months before they saw their actual results on screen. They didn't get early viewings and would be watching all this for the first time along with everyone else when it was screened on TV.

At the start of series two, Neil told the participants that just ten minutes a day would be enough to train their dogs, but he knew they'd need to find their own routines. Different dogs, different terrains and different climates would all play a part in what was achievable. Even just two or three minutes a day, three or four days a week would be a good start. 'Sometimes the training is just having them sit by your chair while you're having a beer,' Neil told them. 'It doesn't all have to be with the livestock.' But he was adamant about one thing. 'Dogs are better off with ten one-minute sessions than simply one ten-minute session. It's very achievable if you discipline yourself.'

One of the difficulties for the participants was what Rob Tuncks calls the chicken and egg scenario. 'You've got to have good calm livestock to train the dog and you can't have calm livestock unless you've got a good dog. And you can't have a good dog unless you've got calm livestock. See what I mean?'

So what did Rob do to get around that?

'Well, I brought in some sheep that had already been trained when I started educating the young pups,' he said. 'The other way to do it is to buy an old mature dog that can control the livestock and then bring a pup in so it's following the old dog's lead. So there are two ways you can do it, but very few people can go with uneducated stock and a young pup and successfully train the dog. Very few people could pull that off.'

One of the most valuable lessons Aticia Grey learned in series one was to understand how things appeared from the pup's perspective. 'Keep in mind that their eyes are below your knee level, and they're going to be seeing your feet first. We wave our arms around up high but that's way above their eyeline, especially if they're concentrating on stock. They're not going to be paying as much attention as you think, which is why we incorporate the rake. It's just an arm extension, but it allows us to put the rake down at the dog's eye level and you can then manoeuvre them around with that.'

At progressive milestones, each of the participants had to show Neil and Helen they could manage the quarter bubble, then half bubble and ultimately the full bubble. It was all about keeping the stock in a calm group.

Neil explained the bubble concept to me later that day in the yard where he holds a lot of his training schools. It was about an hour before sunset and there was a crackling fire burning in a drum inside the shed we'd just left and I was hoping it'd still be going when we were done. There were half a dozen dogs straining on their chains and Neil released one of them. 'Come on, Pup,' he said. Helen had already admitted that with so many dogs coming through, you sometimes just run out of good original names so I suppressed a smile when Neil spoke sternly to 'Pup'.

It was only just becoming clear to me that the fences in a quarter and a half bubble are meant to represent other dogs in a team. 'Those fences are artificially holding the mob because the idea of a full bubble is too much for a pup's comprehension initially,' Neil said. When you've got a pup just starting out, you'll train them in the quarter bubble, and they get used to the idea that they can hold a mob in place. The trainer mob of goats that Neil had were so well practised they followed him around the yard, but Pup thought he was doing the hard work.

'Imagine you're blowing a bubble through a plastic toy,' Neil said, and then tried to make it even simpler for me. 'If you go into the bathroom and put detergent in a bubble pipe and puff a bubble into the air and there's no wind, that bubble will hover there,' he said in between issuing short stern instructions to Pup. 'If you pat the air at the right spot near the bubble, you can push it and control it. If you pat too far from it, it floats and does nothing. If you pat too close, the bubble bursts. It's the same for dogs and livestock. The dogs have got to be aware of where the edge of the bubble is. Too far away and you don't shift the mob; too close and you spill them and they scatter.'

Back inside the shearing shed, he gave me the rake and brought in a dog called Chee, and set me to work. I had to get Chee moving half a dozen wet sheep who'd been brought in from the rain. Neil was telling me which way to wave the rake, but I was confusing myself. It's counterintuitive to point the rake in the direction you don't want the dog to go. Chee, despite his patience, was clearly realising he was working with an amateur. I ended up with wet jeans as the sheep pushed and shoved around me, and I happily retired and gave myself a 'fail'.

Like me, not all of the participants would get a pass for each milestone test. But it would be the finale that truly mattered.

*

Snow was a goofy puppy. If there was a hay bale to jump on or a motorbike within reach, the border collie would leap onto it with all the enthusiasm he could muster and inevitably fall flat on his bottom.

Lily, our participant from Wilcannia, would have a laugh at her dog and wonder if he was doing it on purpose. 'He was pretty clumsy for a while, to be honest, until he worked out what his legs were doing,' she told me. 'He definitely wasn't very graceful. Honestly, if he was around the yard he'd be flapping around like a big long-leggy dog. On the flipside he was pretty cruisy and easy-going.'

Catching up with our participants to check how they were coping with the milestone tasks was always hit and miss. They might have been about to become a modified version of a reality TV star, but they still had jobs to do, farm work to complete and families to take into consideration. Lily was often on the road pursuing mustering contracts. So when I got her on the phone, our conversations would often start in staccato style, partly because of the poor phone connection to outback New South Wales but also due to Lily's modesty. She insisted she was 'crap at explaining things' to me, even though her talent and knowledge easily shone through.

Lily had been a reluctant starter with the *Muster Dogs* series and hadn't had any trouble keeping her involvement a secret, as requested by the producers. With a colourful turn of phrase, she put it this way: 'Oh no, I have told as little people as possible because I am shitting myself since it hit me about being in the public eye. I know that must sound stupid because I signed up to a TV show but I just don't want the publicity!'

Despite her hesitancy, Lily was eager to tackle the early milestones. Not every dog and owner hit it off, but she was fond of Snow straight away and they developed the bluetooth bond that Neil needed to witness. 'Snow was pretty willing to please and at that age I want him coming to me when he hears his name,' she said.

Lily usually has female dogs, with quite a few kelpies in the mix, so to have a male border collie was new territory for her and the rest of her canine team. 'I was always happy with how he was going, and he was doing what I was expecting for that age, but we had to get to understand each other.'

That early bonding meant they easily handled their initial milestones tests. Snow quickly learned how to sit on command, and dragging the 3-metre lead was a breeze. The next milestone test at seven months was another quick pass for Lily. Snow walked with a lead easily and soon matured and lost the gangly features that made him appear so 'kooky'.

Neil's advice that just ten minutes of training a day could make all the difference had sounded doable at the start, but Lily found it tough. She had a trainer mob to practise with at home in Wilcannia, but she spent more time on contracting jobs than she did at home and Snow wasn't ready to be part of her working dog team. He was still only a pup and she didn't want to put him at risk by mixing him with uneducated livestock while she was on the road. 'There was no trainer mob around when I was working,' she said, 'but I kept teaching him the basics and the day-to-day stuff, even if there weren't sheep around. And besides, he got to travel with me.'

One of Lily's biggest challenges with Snow was something she had absolutely no control over – his colour. Snow, as his name suggests, is a predominantly white dog (with black ears) and he had to overcome the livestock's lack of respect for him. 'Because he's white, he doesn't have a lot of presence. He has a bit of trouble shifting the sheep if they're a bit doughy [sluggish] or they might be stubborn. They definitely don't move off him as they do the other coloured dogs,' she explained, referring to the way livestock move as a dog begins mustering them up. Instead, they'd look at Snow defiantly and wonder who'd made him boss. All Lily could do was encourage her snow-white worker to be a bit pushier.

Lily and Snow moved through the milestones with ease but there were still some hiccups. Lily started her pup on the front of the motorbike to get him used to jumping up and travelling with her. He became so adept at this that when she tried to show him that dogs belong on the back of the bike, Snow baulked. 'He wanted to stay up front, but he's quite big. And when you're trying to turn a bit tight, I end up hitting him with the handlebars, so it's getting hard to manoeuvre the bike with him on the front.'

Lily was anticipating that she would do well in the crucial ten-month assessment, but there was an unexpected challenge that morning, just as the camera crew were preparing to film her putting Snow through his paces.

'I headed out to get the trainer mob and discovered that most of them had somehow escaped out of the little paddock they live in,' she told me. 'So that was a bit of a spanner in the works. I tried to get another mob, but they hadn't been educated with dogs.'

She managed to track down the trainer mob and get them back, but their little adventure meant they'd already walked 5 kilometres, so by the time they had to show a bit of movement under Snow's guidance, they were over it. 'They were tired and harder for Snow to move so it didn't go so well,' Lily said.

In the lead-up to the assessment, Lily had been working Snow on bigger mobs so reckoned he might have done well if he'd had more livestock to muster. The crew who filmed them that day thought it was another case of Lily being her own harshest critic.

With the final assessment to be filmed in Queensland a couple of months after we chatted, Lily told me she was setting more goals: to get Snow pushing sheep through gates and mustering sheep on different types of country, and getting him to bark at the right time. I've seen Helen get her dogs to bark by simply saying, 'Speak, speak,' as they jump along the backs of sheep in a narrow pen. Something so simple, though, has only come about because of hours of training.

Lily turned 22 while on a contract mustering job near Tibooburra in far northern New South Wales, about a five-hour drive from her home. There was no cake or celebration, just another day of hard work on the land, working sheep.

Luckily, training Snow had never felt like a chore for her. How could it, when she was doing something she loved? But as the participants headed towards the final days of filming, the anxiety was starting to kick in. 'I'm worried about what people are going to say and think about me doing it, because it's the whole reality TV thing, even though it's nothing like all the other reality TV shows,' she said in her soft voice. 'And I hate the effing cameras.'

'Are you the kind of person who'd rather fly under the radar?' I asked her.

'I dunno. I just do me,' she said, before darting off to her next job.

*

Russ remembers when he got the notes detailing what his dog would have to achieve through the series. 'My first thoughts were, *I'm really gonna have to work on my approach to this,* and *I'll probably have to do a fair bit more work on myself to get up to scratch.'*

The Tasmanian had always thought himself capable, and he took pride in the fact that the team of farmhands helping with his lamb marking would debate which dogs of his were their favourites. 'I've put a lot of time into my dogs, and I think that's where a lot of people go wrong because they're so busy.'

He bonded within a couple of weeks with Molly, who communicated back to him with a head tilt and the prick of her ears, demonstrating the bluetooth connection that Neil required. 'That's the thing I really noticed with her, just the level of intelligence and how quickly she'd pick up on things,' Russ said. 'I'd only have to show it a couple of times and then *bang* she'd have it.'

Bonding seems so simple but can be lost in the mix of a new pup. Aticia from series one reckons the most important thing is to make it fun. 'You're basically taking the pup to school shortly, but preschool is all about having fun and enjoying it and getting prepared for school,' she told me. 'So learn how to have that bond with the pup and interact with them in a way that makes them feel secure.'

With the bonding milestone nailed, Russ raced through the other tasks and was ahead of where he needed to be. The cameras didn't bother him because he felt Molly was capable of everything she was asked to do, although he noticed she was quieter than other dogs he'd owned. 'Molly's an eye dog, like one hundred per cent,' he said, referring to the way she stares down the stock, 'whereas I've always had dogs with a bit of bark or presence.' Molly was good at getting in position and then holding that position. But she was unsure about when and how to come forward and apply pressure to the livestock.

All the participants in series two have told me at one point or another that their dogs have a 'goofy' side to their personalities. I'm not sure it's a trait Mick Hudson would be advertising as part of his breeding brand, but it does mean there are some funny moments. When Molly was six months old, the Fowlers had Russ's extended family over for Boxing Day lunch in the garden. His sisters had come down from Melbourne and the table was groaning under the weight of the feast – potato salad, snags, bread, hamburgers and drinks. 'Rosie let Molly off her leash and she just got so excited about the party, she launched herself onto the table. She just thought, *I'll jump up here and say hello*. Luckily she landed at the other end and we saved the food.' One of the milestones requires the dogs to be comfortable jumping – Russ just hadn't anticipated it would be into their lunch.

Despite that near-disaster, Molly progressed well. At least, until the ten-month milestone and the attempt to round up the sheep. 'So initially when we got out there with the drone flying overhead she whipped around and brought them all to me. *Bang*. Nailed it,' Russ said proudly, when I caught up with him after the assessment. 'Then we had to do it again for the low shot, and then for the wide shot, and I had a couple of pig-headed sheep in there that would stamp their feet and come at the dog, telling her they weren't going to take her orders.'

This was exactly what I saw on the footage with the McDonalds at their farm and why they marked Russ down. But it had a longer-term impact than just half a point on a test. Russ reckoned Molly lost her confidence. 'They didn't want to play ball and then Molly didn't want to get in there. I pulled the pig-headed sheep out, but it was too late and Molly never got back to the same standard she was at the start when she was fresh.'

I wasn't sure what to say other than a lame 'That's a bummer,' because this was a decisive moment for Russ and Molly, and he would have been kicking himself that he didn't just remove those 'pig-headed sheep' from the start. 'She's a great yard work dog but not a paddock dog,' he mused. 'She'll work two or three sheep with confidence, but those bigger mobs throw her. I've just got to make sure she's got other dogs there to help her.'

Russ had applied to be a *Muster Dogs* participant mostly for his little son, Charlie, who had watched series one again and again. On the eve of the crew's arrival to shoot each milestone, Charlie would ask his mum, Rosie, a professional hairdresser, for a haircut so he could look his best. 'When we started, he would be in so many of the shots,' Russ said, remembering the excitement bursting from Charlie's body. 'And he'd be great repeating things whenever Monica or Sally, the other producer, needed another shot. But then he turned four and started being a bit cool for school, which was a shame.'

There was one other thing on Russ's mind at that ten-month mark. He knew the finale was going to be held at Frank Finger's cattle property near Clermont in central Queensland. 'It's not just Molly going into a different environment, you know. I've never been to Queensland either!' he told me. He'd been taking Molly to his neighbour's farm to get her used to working something other than sheep. 'I might have to do some practice in a big shed with the heater on to get her used to the Queensland climate,' he said with a laugh. 'Rosie always gets into me and thinks I'm not excited, but I am; I'm just trying to be cool, calm and collected. I know that if I get up there with Molly and I'm nervous, that will affect her.'

Whatever was to happen in the finale, Russ was glad he took the gamble in signing up. 'Just having that lightbulb moment, to learn that I can change the mindset of the sheep in how I use the dogs – instead of the sheep getting spooked and running and pushing over fences and hurting themselves, they're so calm. Neil calls it "making them dickhead-proof", so you can have cars tooting and cowboys in there cracking whips, but they stay in that nice mellow state. I've got the techniques now to fix problems.'

*

Cilla, the would-be cattle baron in southeast Queensland, had a couple of helpers at eye level – her children. Although, if anything, Greta and Annie were possibly too helpful; so desperate to be part of the fun with Ash, the border collie, they sometimes threatened to derail the training.

Cilla started this process wracked with self-doubt, knowing the other participants were probably more experienced. But both she and Ash built up their confidence rapidly. 'I'm really proud of her,' she said after the seven-month milestone assessment. 'She did everything I asked her to do, so if anything was not right it's on me for instructing her incorrectly.' In fact, Cilla was amazed at how Ash Barky did, given the distractions. 'There are different people here today. There are cameras and there are sound guys with weird things and then there are the drones!'

It reminded me of an experience I had in 2016 filming for the ABC in the United Kingdom at a time when Britons were still debating whether to exit the European Union. An ABC camera operator and I caught the train from London to the Welsh university town of Aberystwyth, which is fondly known as Aber to its population of 13,000. It was about a seven-hour journey door to door, and we had to factor in extra time to lug the camera gear round.

I'd chosen to do some interviews in the area because it was known for its sheep farms and its European export industry. In fact, opinion polls had declared it the most pro-EU region in the UK, and with just months until the Brexit vote I was curious about how they were feeling. I was also tempted by the fact that I'd get to sign off a story with 'Lisa Millar, ABC News, Aberystwyth, Wales'. There's nothing like nailing a Welsh tongue twister of a location to make you feel you've achieved something.

The farmer we'd been planning to meet, Rhodri Lloyd-Williams, lived just outside of town. Moelgolomen Farm was nestled in the Cambrian Mountains and, like most of the producers in the area, Rhodri didn't have a lot of land – just 300 hectares – on which he ran his 800 organic Welsh Mountain ewes. The rolling green hills provided a stunning backdrop and, as we bounced along the potholed dirt road in his old four-wheel drive, Rhodri told us that on a clear day you could almost see Ireland.

He'd rung me that morning to tell me he had a terrible head cold and was feeling miserable. But he knew we'd come a long way to film, so he'd go ahead with the interview if we were quick – a promise we readily made. He'd already rounded up his sheep to the top of the mountain where we wanted to film the beautiful vista. The cameraman asked him to hold off moving them into the next paddock for a moment until he could get the drone up. I probably don't need to tell you what happened next: the minute the drone lifted up and those rotors hovered overhead, a hundred sheep literally ran for the hills, and I thought we'd reduce poor sick Rhodri to tears.

It's remarkable that the drones used by the *Muster Dogs* film crews didn't have the same effect on any of our participants, their dogs or the livestock they'd been working. But Cilla told me she was ready for things to fall apart on any given day. So far, Ash had proven to be very focused, but Cilla wouldn't know until the finale how her dog compared to others from the litter. 'Her control is really the one thing I'm very proud of. She's still exercising self-control when she's excited and wanting to do something, but she's waiting for the cue.'

Cilla came into the experiment after a rough few years and she knew she'd be up against it – trying to train a working dog while raising three children and running the farm was not going to be a picnic. 'Ash has taught me a lot about myself actually,' she reflected. 'Observance and dedication, for starters. I've got to show this dog what I need her to do, but she's showing me my strengths. And she's showing me my weaknesses too, and that's what makes the team. I keep saying the more I learn, the less I feel I know because it's just getting bigger and bigger and more exciting as we go.'

She considered herself a rookie and hoped she was doing Ash justice. She'd thrown herself into this challenge and had put hundreds of hours of time into training Ash but still wondered, *Is it enough? Have I done enough?* 'And there's a very delicate line between asking just the right amount, knocking off at the right time so that your doggy is still excited about what you're doing once more and not saying, "Not again. Do we really have to do it again, Mum?"'

Because Cilla's a performer at heart as well as a farmer, she tried to record her training sessions so she could review them. 'You can pick up on so many things that other people are seeing, that your doggy is seeing, but you don't understand at the time. So being able to tweak as you go has been important.' The mission to turn Ash into a champion was turning into an obsession, she readily admitted. 'I watch dog training videos, I read dog training books, I have dog training dreams!'

Winter was late coming to Ban Ban Springs. They got a little unexpected rain, and the grass grew before the cooler months started. It was a good season for farming. But Cilla had been spending all her waking hours wondering what else she needed to do to get Ash ready for the finale. In a sign of just how determined she is, she decided to pack up the kids and drive three hours north to take part in a training school with Joni Hall from series one.

'Scott stayed home but I took the kids plus a babysitter and it was hectic,' she told me, with a few expletives thrown in to describe her level of exhaustion by the end of it. 'I was trying to make Ash more bold with the cattle, so doing the road trip to see Joni was brilliant. I'm a huge fan of Joni's and what she does. She's funny, she's great, she's relaxed about working the dogs. She doesn't take it too seriously. And I tend to take things too seriously. So it was great for me. Joni's always saying, "Just have fun."

'Joni actually got Ash so annoyed that the stock weren't doing what she wanted that she let out this little bark of frustration. And – oh! – it was so exciting to hear that bark because the stock moved off and Ash felt this power and I felt this power on her behalf.'

The camera crew returned to Ban Ban Springs for the ten-month assessment and Cilla had to prove she could keep the bluetooth connection with Ash despite distractions. They both lay on the grass in the house yard while the three children, including her toddler, Sidney, ran past in a gust of giggles, followed by Minty, the little fluffy shih-tzu. Ash rolled over, letting her eyes follow the tiny crew, but then rolled back to Cilla, her body never leaving the ground. 'I gave her the rules and she stuck to them, but she just bent them a tiny bit.' Thankfully Neil and Helen decided it was a pass.

Cilla was feeling stressed as the weeks passed and the finale loomed. She told me that she went to a naturopath who gave her a calming tonic to help keep her heart rate steady and to stop her burning up energy. She thought it was working until Greta, her four-year-old, asked one day if she'd taken her 'calm medicine'.

'I said to her, "Yes, darling, I have," and she goes, "Well, why are you yelling then?"' She snorted with laughter remembering the moment. 'The kids are good at keeping you in check, but I did think, *Dammit, why am I yelling?*'

Keeping her own anxiety at bay would help Cilla build Ash's confidence for the next couple of months. And they needed to fine-tune any areas of training that they might have glossed over. 'For example, she's got a very direct cast,' Cilla said, describing how much room Ash put between herself and the stock as she ran around them. 'Ideally, I'd like her to give the stock a little more room because that gives her more options.' They were working with educated predictable stock and Cilla knew she'd have to challenge Ash a little more. 'It may be a bit trickier than what I anticipated because up to this point I thought I would be able to get her to cast wider than I have, and I haven't nailed that. When she goes to take off, you want to put physical pressure onto the dog by blocking them from coming directly towards the stock. I'm going to use an arm extension that makes a noise, like a stick with a noisy bag on the end, to get her to take off more squarely so that she heads out before she heads in.'

It sounded complicated but Cilla had been plotting this path in her dreams at night, even if she wasn't sure how it would turn out. 'It'll probably involve a lot of me running around the paddock yahooing and carrying on so she still sees me and keeps me in the picture but remains focused on the stock. It's probably not going to be very glamorous,' she said with a laugh.

I asked her what she hoped Neil and Helen would think when they saw Ash in action. 'I'm really hoping that they see what I see, and that is the champion little doggie. And I hope that I'm not letting the team down. I hope that they see lots of improvement in me too.'

Cilla's involvement in *Muster Dogs* went beyond a desire to see if she could train a dog properly. She wanted to prove something to her family as well. Returning from the city to the country hadn't been a difficult decision, but having her country family accept that she was there for keeps had proved more difficult. Her brothers are both excellent stockmen and she's spent a lifetime living in their shadow.

'I think, on a really personal level, this process has given me the chance to get better at a craft, get better at being a stock handler, a stockwoman, a farmer – and building confidence to actually put my name to it and say, yes, I am a fourth-generation grazier and, yes, I can do it because here's the proof,' she said emphatically. 'It's becoming more obvious to me as this process goes forward that not only do I love it, I can actually do it. And hopefully do it really well. I'm excited for the rest of my journey as a grazier.'

*

Across the country Zoe Miller wasn't thinking about training her dog, Buddy, at all. She was just trying to keep him alive. They'd been on the road in the Northern Territory when she noticed he'd vomited up the food she'd put out that morning.

'Right from the beginning when I first got him as a puppy he's been really delicate with food and I had to change what I gave him,' she told me. 'But I didn't panic because I thought, well, he's delicate when travelling, and it's not completely out of character for him to throw up.'

By the time they got home to Katherine, a few hours' drive away, he seemed to have improved and she was able to get him back on his regular diet. But still nothing seemed to go right. A new bag of dog food was mouldy when she opened it so she shifted him to other dog food; then he was throwing up again. 'I got him into the vet and it's been an ordeal since. Well, maybe not an ordeal, but definitely a process.'

Working dogs don't carry a lot of weight. They're active and burn through the fuel they ingest. But Buddy was skinny, too skinny, and Zoe knew something wasn't right. He was on medication and seemed to be improving but then he came home from the vet and he went back downhill. 'So then I tried him with different food to see if he had an allergy or just a sensitivity reaction but, right now, I've got him back at the vet and he seems to be always nauseous.'

It broke Zoe's heart to see him wagging his tail when he saw her, bright and happy, even though he was clearly so sick. 'It *is* heartbreaking. You keep them up to date with their worming tablets, you vaccinate them, you try to cover all your bases. Even the vets say, "I just wish they could talk to us and tell us what's going on."'

The reality is that dogs get sick and injured. Mustering can be dangerous. The puppies weren't wrapped in cotton wool during the year they were being filmed for the *Muster Dogs* program; they were hard at work. And, of course, eventually, dogs simply just get old.

As Rob memorably said in series one, 'The only thing dogs do wrong is they don't live long enough.' Anyone who has lost a dog would have felt the sadness emanating from him as he described what had happened to his long-time companion, a dog called Jumpy. We'd all watched Rob's face lighting up whenever she was nearby. As an older dog she'd been allowed into the house, and it was there on the kitchen floor that she collapsed. For that moment on screen Rob was no longer the joker of the series but the truthteller. 'Farmers really do get attached to their dogs, we love them, despite how tough we might act.'

Farming *is* risky – we haven't even spoken yet about the snakes, not always visible but a constant presence, especially for the film crew who had to squeeze into position to get the best shot. Monica's husband, DOP Brad Smith, had a close encounter in series one. They were filming in the stockyards with Joni and her dog, Chet, when Brad jumped over the fence to get down low to get the dog's perspective pushing against the cattle.

'I dropped to the ground, and I was trying to punch lower and lower to get the lens under the second bottom rail to get right next to the dog and I could feel this sensation of something wriggling under my knee,' he told me, his body shuddering at the thought. 'And I look down between my two knees and there's this copper brown colour. I mean, everywhere was snake. I looked to the left and there was snake and I looked to the right and there was snake, and underneath me there was snake.'

It was a 3-metre-long olive python, harmless to humans but seriously traumatising for Brad. He couldn't remember much more but the sound recordist Jerry Batha could – he captured Brad's screams and played them to me later for full effect.

'F***, Jesus Christ, I've got a python under me, for f***'s sake, Jesus f***ing Christ, for f***'s sake.' And so the audio went on, Brad's squeals becoming higher and higher with each expletive. You can hear Jerry's laughter on the soundtrack. 'I couldn't help it,' Jerry said. 'I've never seen someone react like that.'

The olive python might be harmless, but there are plenty of other venomous snakes ready to take down a working dog. Zoe knew Buddy hadn't been bitten, though, and she and the vet were mystified as to what was wrong. She couldn't contemplate the thought of losing him, not after the months of training and the bond they'd formed. 'My good friend said I might have jinxed myself by calling him Buddy because he's presenting like a bit of a delicate rosebud.'

Buddy's illness struck again just as the film crew arrived to witness the ten-month milestone attempt. Monica sent me photos and we both had a sinking feeling – *What if Buddy died at this point in the series?* It would be devastating and not something we would want to have to share with viewers.

They ruled out any attempt at the ten-month milestones.

'Because of the weight he was, I was already thinking we weren't going to be able to do it,' Zoe told me. 'There's no way I'd ask a dog to work in that condition. And this was going to be more physically strenuous.'

It was clear Buddy was a very special addition into her team. 'I just love him, he's full of confidence with old soul eyes,' Zoe told the film crew. He was home from the vet, but he was exhausted. 'He's just so tired, you can see it's taken a toll on him.'

They'd done well through their previous milestones; even when, at the last minute, she had to substitute goats that had been trained differently to the mob she'd planned on using. 'One of the goats broke away during the full bubble but Buddy got around and brought it back really neatly. He's got some great ability.'

She knew, though, it was the right decision to skip the ten-month assessment. She'd just have to see how far they'd both come when they joined the other participants in Queensland for the finale.

It wasn't the only emotional toll Zoe was facing. Her relationship of seven years had ended. She'd started this *Muster Dogs* journey with a partner and now she was going it alone. It would be hard enough for anyone but to be going through that in front of a film crew was even tougher. When I'd spoken to Zoe a few months earlier on a video call, she was a picture of 'togetherness'. She'd appeared in front of me on the screen, her hair neatly tied back in a bun, a small scarf around her neck to ward off the sun and dust, bright pearls in her ears. But she revealed she sometimes felt like an imposter. It was her old struggle with self-confidence.

At the ten-month mark, she told Monica she'd often thought of calling Neil McDonald to give him a friendly scolding for suggesting she take part in the show in the first place. 'Because there are so many other people who can train a dog better. Sometimes I feel a bit guilty that I got this opportunity.'

Monica sat with her outside her home in Katherine, a home she was preparing to leave for good, and gave her a hug. 'You need to cut yourself a break, young lady,' she told Zoe warmly. 'You've put in so much effort and you've got big, clear plans.'

Zoe didn't know how the next two months before the finale would unfold but she knew she had work to do, as long as Buddy got better. 'His nature, his trainability, it's unreal where he's at. And he's helped me so much. It's like he had my back, and he was saying, "It's OK, we've got this together." He's a lovely dog to have in the camp. He's very special to me.'

*

Meanwhile, up in Winton, Steve had his dog, Indi, in the round yard at the back of the house, teaching her to 'balance'. He wanted to teach her to push the stock through a gateway or into a yard, rather than gathering them up and bringing them back to him. 'We've all experienced it. You'll have the dogs doing a beautiful job all day long and then you want the animals through a gate and good old stupid Fido goes through and bloody brings them all back to you! The dog thinks the stock are getting away and he doesn't understand fences.'

Indi was showing some promise. She was a ball of fun and wanted to please Steve. But he wasn't getting too carried away; it's not in his nature. Steve was already an experienced dog trainer when he joined *Muster Dogs* and some of the ideas Neil has about training aren't necessarily how Steve has successfully operated over the years. One of the first things he decided not to do as part of the first milestone assessment at five months was the quarter bubble. He thought it could start bad habits. But he didn't want to make a big deal of it, nor appear to be causing division with Neil.

After Steve's accident 20 years ago, he became interested in dog trials and went on to win dozens of awards. He likes the friendship of the circuit and it's something his wheelchair doesn't stop him doing – although he's had the odd comment from other competitors that he's 'fortunate' because the livestock think his wheelchair is a four-wheeler and are intimidated. He's not so sure he's 'fortunate', but he's always trying to improve his trialling skills and his experience has also given him a different perspective going into these milestones. 'You lose points in dog trials with some of these things,' he explains of his decision to avoid the quarter bubble.

I'll admit that in the process of working with the *Muster Dogs* teams on this project I've learned a lot more about dogs than I ever thought I'd need to know. But some aspects got quite complicated fairly quickly. What I was sure of was that Steve was so adamant about standing his ground against the quarter bubble that I wasn't going to question him further on it.

He was also firm on how the dogs are allowed to play. 'A lot of bad habits can be created when you let the dog out of the cage – and playing in the yard, that's where it all starts. People in the city teach their dogs to wiggle through their legs and do circles and it's an awesome thing, but they never have to work stock. They're using their dog for enjoyment.

We're using ours for work,' he said, before adding, 'and enjoyment too.'

He told me it takes two years for a dog to mature, and it can be more than that for it to get 100 per cent of a handle on the commands. And before that, they've got to get through their teenage years, and that can be a frustrating time.

The seven-month assessment arrived with Steve in a good place. There'd been a bit of rain over Christmas, and it hadn't been too hot. The grass was growing, and Winton was looking good. 'Yeah, Indi joined in the Christmas spirit, and she had the reindeer horns on her, and it was fun,' Steve recalled.

Keri's kids loved being part of it all during school holidays. They were quick to name the other pups that Steve had in the cage near the house and they were full of questions for him. Keri said the new pups knew to listen out for the noises of the wheelchair as he headed their way. 'We end up treading on little pups' toes here and there and it only takes them once to learn. It's rare for a second time. When they hear the clicking noise of the chair, they get out of the way pretty quick.'

Steve trains his dogs the same way I imagine an old-style cowboy does it. There's not a lot of time for cuddles and he's not interested in treating them like humans. A dog is a dog. 'What's confusing for a dog is we humanise them. And dogs aren't humans. Animals aren't humans. We've got to start thinking what the dogs think,' he said.

He's perplexed by city folk who go for a walk with their dog towing them along, like their pet is a husky out the front of a sled. 'They get out in front, and they pull like all hell and if they're the leader they're making the decisions. That's what the problem is.' If you want a well-behaved dog, Steve said, you need to have some discipline and a reward at the end. It seems tough but Steve's been doing this a long time and it works for him. But I had a private smile when I spied him later pulling a puppy up onto his wheelchair for a quick squeeze of affection.

Steve's mum was pretty tough. There were four boys in the family and if they ever whinged to her, it was a case of 'Stiff shit, mate, suck it up.' He's philosophical about ending up in a wheelchair. 'That's what I got, that's what I've got to work with. And I always believe it'll work out, no matter what situation you're in.'

With that approach to life, it's no surprise Steve made it through the milestones easily, albeit with a bit of ribbing from Keri along the way. He thought the cameras might have helped Indi. 'Oh, she might be a little show pony. I think she was really switched on. She shifted up to another level.' He was impressed at how she took control when moving the stock to him. 'There's a leader in a mob. A mob will stop all the time and there's always the one that wants to run away. She done real good stopping the one, the main one, from running.'

All along, Steve had been cautious about pushing Indi too quickly. 'It's like a young kid playing football and he's really good with the under-eights, and there's not a big population in town so the under-tens ask him to play. And then everything's going real good and they make him play the under-twelves and he gets smashed. And you don't see him play football no more.'

The analogy is the same for dogs, Steve said. Push them too far, put them in with cattle before they're ready, and they get hurt. And then it takes them a long time to come back from that.

Dig a little deeper with Steve and he'll admit Indi has inspired him. 'It's opened up a whole new world and you don't know what will come from it.'

*

Our participants were all so different to each other: from their backgrounds and experiences, to the stunning parts of Australia they call home. And all had different reasons for taking on the *Muster Dogs* challenge, even if they didn't fully understand what drove them until they were well down the path. These season-two participants had been given beautifully bred border collies and they'd had top-notch trainers on hand for advice. So what would set them apart to determine which dog was named the champion?

CHAPTER 7

That's a Wrap

Hillview was where it would all come to an end, as well as spark a new beginning. Frank Finger's 240,000-hectare property in central Queensland with its big cattle yards and ironbark trees had been selected as the destination for the final week of filming in July.

It was chosen because it was climate neutral and accessible for all participants and the cattle were well educated, allowing for the safest and fairest competition to play out. The Finger family's hospitality was an added bonus.

The mild winter days in Clermont would work for Steve, whose body struggled to cope with extreme heat and cold, and the location, 500 kilometres south of Winton, would make it a smooth five-hour drive for him, Keri and 15 of their dogs.

The *Muster Dogs* journey had been a rollercoaster of emotions for each of the participants as they faced unexpected challenges and hurdles and – for some – a new appreciation of the pressure they could sustain. But who knew that, for some of them, actually getting on the road to put their dogs to the last test would also be a feat of endurance.

Russ – making his first trip to Queensland – was booked to fly from Hobart to Brisbane and onward to Mackay with Rosie and the children. But a leg of the flight was cancelled and they ended up getting stuck in Sydney overnight. To make matters worse, they were separated from pup Molly, who was in the crate they always used to transport her. It was a stressful 24 hours before they were all reunited in Mackay. And it didn't stop there: with all their luggage and Milly's pram in the rental 4WD, they couldn't fit in Molly's crate. So Russ and Rosie left the crate at the airport and hit the road for the three-and-a-half-hour drive to Clermont with Molly propped between the kids' car seats.

'I'm not sure the rental car company would want to know. But, honestly, you wouldn't know she was there unless you said, "Hello, Molly, how are you going?" and she pops her head up from the seat,' Russ told me.

Cilla, who lives 700 kilometres south of Frank's place, broke the trip into two days, to give her three kids and pup Ash a break.

Zoe drove solo, as she often does, from the Northern Territory. It took her three days and it was, at times, frustratingly slow. With three horses, pup Buddy and seven other dogs, a trailer and her four-wheel buggy on the back, she could never do more than 100 kilometres an hour on those outback roads. Luckily, Buddy's health had improved. When he was at his sickest, he'd been able to tolerate tuna and salmon but not much else, so in a world of increasingly finicky eaters, Buddy had been declared a pescatarian – not a common diagnosis in the animal world but one that seemed to help. Dogs certainly suffer from food intolerances and some can become allergic to protein, but normally an allergy shows itself with skin irritation and excessive itching. Thankfully, though, his intolerance was short-lived, and Zoe had been able to start adding chicken and meat back into his diet. He was ready for the finale.

After arriving home from a mustering job the night before, Lily jumped in her ute with Snow and her two kelpies at 6am and spent two days making the trek from Wilcannia.

The border collies' breeders, Mick and Carolyn Hudson, drove for 14 hours from their home in Eumungerie, north of Dubbo in central New South Wales, stopping overnight before arriving on Sunday, 16 July.

But it was our trainers, Neil and Helen McDonald, who faced the longest drive – and definitely the most challenging. They set off from their farm in Keith in South Australia in a convoy of three trucks, a ute with a horse trailer, 83 lambs, six goats, three bulls and 13 dogs. They had 2500 kilometres ahead of them and a whole lot of headaches.

They needed these particular sheep and goats for the final assessments because they were already educated around working dogs, making them predictable for both the participants and the filmmakers. Frank only has cattle on his property, and it would have been too complicated for Neil and Helen to source local sheep in central Queensland.

At 5am in Keith, with the temperature hovering just above zero and the rain falling on their already soaked winter beanies, they were wondering what they'd got themselves into. It was dark and the torchlights were making the lambs disoriented. They baulked at the ramp to the truck, refusing to go up. Neil and Helen had enlisted the help of some friends, and they soon needed it. John, who lives on a property near theirs, was going to join them on the road, along with another friend, Anita, who was 62, tiny in stature and one of the hardest workers they knew. She's a champion horsewoman – the only woman in fact to ever win the famous Rocky Rush Open Stockman's Challenge, and she proudly wears the massive 2007 belt buckle prize around her waist. She'd been recently widowed, and Neil and Helen thought she might enjoy the trip. It didn't hurt that she also had a truck licence. But even with those extra expert hands, getting the lambs loaded took an hour longer than it should have.

They eventually got on the road and, with a few breaks, pulled into their first overnight stop at a mate's property near Wilcannia around 10.30pm. They unloaded the still-reluctant lambs into a yard, fed the dogs and settled in for a few hours' sleep. Helen bunked in the truck with Neil, and John and Anita were in the shearers' quarters.

The next morning, they repeated the process, but waited until daylight to get the lambs back onboard. The departure was speedy this time; the rest of the journey was anything but. It was a catalogue of road dramas. A rear end on one of the trucks collapsed; a diesel tank ran empty unexpectedly; there was no phone service; their UHF radios let them down; a few more mechanical problems struck – and it was a bedraggled, exhausted mob that finally limped into Clermont at midnight four days later. The sheep were happy at least, and ready to play their starring role for the cameras.

I had the easiest journey of the lot – relaxing into my seat on the flight from Melbourne, a couple of days after the others, no kids or animals involved. I was the show's narrator and had no on-camera duties, but I wanted to see firsthand the final day of filming. I caught a nap and discovered when I landed in Emerald, Queensland, that the rental agency had switched my 'cheapest car you've got, please' for a large top-of-the-range 4WD. It was all they had, they explained. There's not a lot of demand, it seems, for economy hatchbacks in the bush.

In Clermont, Monica had still been hoping to keep the individual participants' presence a secret from each other. But in a town of 2500 people with only a couple of options for accommodation for such a big group, it didn't take long for everyone to work out who they were up against. Neil and Helen were staying at Frank's, about 20 minutes outside town, but most of the participants were in the local motel.

There were kids, utes and dogs all coming and going from the motel. Because Russ didn't have a crate for Molly, she bunked in with Ash, Cilla's dog. The two sisters, joyous litter mates back in their Dubbo days, happily curled up together for the first time since their separation around nine months earlier.

There's something warmly nostalgic about a country motel in Australia. Four-wheel drives covered in dust park with their noses just a metre from the door of each room, headlights shining in through thin curtains. We obey the sign that says to leave dirt-covered work boots outside and plop them down near a rusty chair and a ubiquitous ashtray. Grey nomads and contract workers sit outside having a beer, enjoying the last moments of an outback sunset.

Breakfast order forms are ticked – toast, cereal, fried eggs – and left at reception before 7pm. When I was a kid, I thought it was exotic to order the tomato juice that came chilled in a small bottle. The freshly toasted white bread arrives slightly cool and damp, despite being tucked into a small paper bag to keep it warm. Just in case there's any doubt, the bag is decorated with the word 'Toast' in cursive lettering that might have been printed in the 1970s. The eggs and sausages stay hidden under a metal lid, which, when lifted, reveals an obligatory sprig of parsley. 'Look at the effort we've gone to,' that parsley tells me.

In central Queensland, there's a knock at the door signalling breakfast has arrived. But there are still motels in country Australia where a little opening in the wall is unlocked on the outside and the motel owner, who often doubles as the cook, quietly slides the tray inside while you're still tucked up warm in bed. These hatches have disappeared over the years, but I mentioned them once on social media and was immediately flooded with the fond memories of hundreds of motel guests.

Even though Monica gave up on keeping everyone apart, she made them promise one thing – that they wouldn't watch each other's dogs working livestock. Each of them had been allocated specific training times at Frank's farm to get used to the yards and the stock they'd be using for the assessments.

This final week of filming was a huge operation for the *Muster Dogs* crew, especially Ben Emery, the director of photography. He'd witnessed the excitement, fun and chaos through the lens of the series-one finale in the sweltering heat of the Northern Territory, so he was an old hand by now.

This time the number of camera operators was boosted to five, plus assistants and a stills photographer. They were using nine cameras including three drones and half a dozen GoPros. Monica had convinced Jerry Batha, the sound recordist on series one, to come out of retirement for the week and join Ash Eden, bumping the sound team up to two operators. Each day they would be attaching microphones to a dozen people, strapping battery packs around stomachs and securing leads under shirts to make sure nothing would be visible to the cameras. Their headphones would never be far from their ears as they listened to voices and barking and the sounds of hooves to ensure nothing would be missed.

Monday, 17 July arrived, and the participants gathered in front of the cameras as a group for the first time. After weeks of unseasonable rain, the skies had cleared and the dawn arrived with the promise of another perfect day. It was a crisp morning but nothing compared to what Russ was used to in Tasmania; Molly was the only dog among the siblings that had ever frolicked in snow. As he looked around at the group, this farmer from Bothwell felt humbled. 'It sunk in then and I thought, *Oh shit, Steve has trained dogs for years. Gee, I've really got to get it on here.*'

On that first day of filming, participants met at the dam and were interviewed about their journeys up to that point. The shoot was a success and everything was on schedule. And at a barbecue that evening, Carolyn and Mick turned up and surprised everyone. The dogs had still been puppies when Carolyn had tearfully farewelled them all those months before, but they clearly hadn't forgotten her. They nuzzled in for a pat, straining at their leads.

But the next two days would be more challenging as each of the dogs was put through its paces.

The first task involved moving a mob of goats through two lines of barrels that were approximately 3 metres apart. That distance was narrowed between each run as the challenge progressed. Eventually there was just a metre gap that the participants had to manoeuvre the mob through. Neil explained it like this: 'You walk ahead and you have a garden rake or a noodle, and if a dog comes down too far on one side you block it. And if it comes down too far on the other side you block it. It's very important how you walk and lead your stock around.'

As the barrels were brought in closer, the participants had to move more fluidly and be observant while not staring too much at their dog. 'You've got to make your rake work, you've got to have your voice work, and if an animal breaks away [from the mob] then you're out,' Neil explained. They'd have to then sit and watch as the others tackled the narrower barrels.

The next task was designed to simulate an approaching flood or bushfire. There were 16 sheep in a yard and the participants had to get them to safety and onto a horse float as quickly as possible. There were no rules about how they were moved, but it had to be done in a careful manner. 'You can go to the left, the right or you can do spins or have a bag in your hand, as long as it is careful and swift,' Neil said. This was not Molly's finest moment. The Tasmanian dog wasn't used to working in yards and kept knocking off the job. In the end Russ was left to get the sheep into the trailer by himself – his working dog deciding work was not for her.

In the final task, the border collies and their trainers were tested on their mustering skills. They had to move a mob of 15 cows over a distance of 200 metres, from outside a set of yards and through a gate. The participants had to ensure their dog would go around and block the mob so they didn't start running away.

Russ and Molly had developed a tight bond during their time together, but Carolyn's presence at the finale changed the dynamic. Molly had been Carolyn's favourite pup, and even though months had passed, there was still a strong connection between them. Molly kept wandering away from her tasks to look for love from the woman whose kitchen she'd been born in and who'd cared for her for her first few months of life. Carolyn felt bad for Russ, but he took it in his stride.

Steve had his own problem to deal with – a flat tyre on his wheelchair. He'd been forced to leave it in town for repairs and switch to his two-wheeler, similar to a Segway. 'I picked up a nail in the carpark,' he said, characteristically resisting any fuss. 'No big deal. Wouldn't have made a difference to the results.' I asked him which wheel had the flat, and Steve, always the joker, replied, 'The driver's side', before pushing the button under his hand and rolling off. Steve's friend Keri had been a big part of the *Muster Dogs* journey and, although her dog Bobby wasn't part of the litter, they participated in the assessments along the way. They held their own during the finale and Neil declared during one task, 'That's my kind of dog. I like his work style.'

Monica, Michael Boughen and the production team, along with trainers Helen and Neil, had designed the three tasks to show the different skills you'd want to see in a working dog. When filming got underway, it became apparent that, despite the pups' excellent breeding, none of them had the force the trainers had been anticipating at this point, perhaps a sign of the difference between kelpies and border collies. So they modified the tasks along the way to make sure the young dogs weren't pushed too hard.

Just as in the first series, the concept behind the show was to see if a working dog could be trained in just one year, as opposed to the industry expectation of three years. All the tasks the pups were set were designed to assess their ability in relation to everything they had learned over the year-long experiment.

The barrel and goat task demonstrated their ability to work on balance.

Getting the sheep into the trailer demonstrated their ability to work off balance.

And rounding up the cattle demonstrated their ability to mob the stock up and drive them across a distance.

And there was one requirement in common across all three tasks: a deep bond, connection, trust and intuition between the handler and the pup.

But only one of these five pairs could be the champion and as the skies darkened on the last afternoon of filming on Wednesday, the judges were still struggling with how close the competition was. They'd be announcing the winner the next day and pondered if they should spend some time going over the footage before they made their final decision. It was clearly weighing on them.

I got into town that afternoon, and I checked into the local motel around 5pm. My journey from Melbourne might have been easy, but I'd still been awake since 3am, thanks to my regular day's work hosting breakfast TV. I decided to lie down on the motel bed for 'just a moment' and woke an hour later to a hubbub of voices outside as everyone returned from filming the final assessment at Frank's. Stories were being shared, so too beer and vodka. The hard part was over, the assessments all complete. Now it was just up to the judges to decide who would be named champion Muster Dog. I'd spent hours on calls with the participants over the previous five months, and even though I was meeting some of them face to face for the first time, it felt like a catchup with old friends.

They told me what had happened that afternoon – another surprise for all of them.

They'd been sitting under a tree, discussing the events of the day for the cameras, when Frank Finger quietly walked up behind Mick with a pure white dog on a lead. It was Lucky – the deaf puppy from the same litter as their pups. Mick and Carolyn had given Lucky to Frank nine months earlier, but Mick didn't know Frank had been training him to become a working dog. The other participants didn't even know he existed.

Not only was Lucky doing well, Frank told them, but he also had a girlfriend called Flo – and the two of them were happy little working dogs who could muster cattle with the best of them. Flo would hear Frank's commands and would let her deaf pal know what they needed to do. It was an emotional moment for everyone, and the only time Mick Hudson was genuinely left speechless.

Later at the motel, the participants laughed as they recalled Mick's shocked face, and with each drink the story gathered embellishment. They all went to bed that night relieved the hard work was over but not knowing if they'd managed to pull off an upset at the end of their year-long experiment. Whose dog would be declared champion? The anticipation was part of the icing on the cake – together with the satisfaction of making it to the finish line.

Russ was the only one who was resigned to the outcome. Molly was a top dog in his eyes, but she just hadn't nailed some of the tasks and he knew she was out of the race.

Steve reckoned that even if Indi didn't come up as the champion, there were other wonderful compensations. 'What a beautiful bunch of people to be working with,' he said. 'And if you had to go and do a job with any of those dogs you wouldn't be afraid to take any of them.'

Thursday, 20 July dawned cool and clear. The call time for the crew was extra early – 6.15am. This day would be the culmination of months of planning and Monica wanted it to be seamless. There was just a hint of the spectacular sunrise to come as the cavalcade of cars left the motel on time and headed for Frank's property.

They'd chosen a filming spot not far from the original farmhouse, constructed by Frank's parents in the 1940s. It was all but abandoned now, apart from an occasional farm visitor throwing a mattress on the floor. The cattle yards had been built by Frank and his brother 30 years before using timber from the property. They could fit 500 head of cattle in there. Every month of the year there'd be something going on – calf branding, vet checks, medical treatments, weaners to take off their mothers. But on this morning, the yards were empty and the air was still. Even the leaves on the hardwood ironbarks, standing tall around the property, barely moved.

The crew began the meticulous operation of setting up for the final shoot. Ben did a walk-through with one of the shooters – as the camera operators are known in the industry – checking the path of the sunlight onto the patch of grass they wanted to use. They set up a two-storey-high bounce board – which in reality is a piece of fabric specifically created to reflect light. It was so big it had to be harnessed to the trees like a mainsail on a yacht. Camera positions were plotted and lenses chosen; they needed wide angles for the big group scenes and long lenses for tight shots of people's faces and their reactions to the big reveal.

Cameras were loaded, time codes were synchronised, and they asked a few people to pretend to be the participants so they could tweak the shots. Ten members of the crew, including Monica, had earpieces firmly in place, communicating through a secure digital radio system.

Monica and co-producer Michael ran through the process with Neil and Helen, who would take the lead in announcing the winners. We'd teased Neil over the months of filming about his predilection for tracksuit pants, loose wool slippers and beanies, but that day both he and Helen were in collared shirts – Helen's bright red and white spots standing out among the browns and greens of the cattle yard. In a sign of how mild the Queensland winter weather was, Steve was wearing shorts; a vest over his blue checked shirt was the only nod to the season.

And then it was time. The participants took their positions: Steve, Cilla, Russ, Lily and Zoe. Their dogs, the stars of the show, were a little restless – standing to attention initially, then flopping down to the ground as the process dragged on. We knew the final product, once it aired, would be emotional, intense and dramatic. But getting there could be frustratingly slow for 'talent' (as we call the stars) who didn't spend every waking hour in TV land.

They were given one last reminder to tip their hats so the wide brims didn't hide their faces from the cameras. Helen cleared her throat and Monica called out, 'Quiet on set.' Each of the camera operators was rolling and it was time for Helen to announce the winner. It had been such a difficult decision that Helen sounded almost apologetic as she stumbled over her words, explaining how well each dog had performed and emphasising the tightness of the outcome. But there could only be one champion.

'And that is Zoe with Buddy,' Helen declared.

Zoe smiled tentatively before she dropped her head to give Buddy's ears a gentle tug. In her blue jeans and aqua shirt and scarf, her red hair tucked under a battered broad-brimmed hat, she looked the picture of country.

'It's a great credit to you, Zoe, because you've gone through a lot within this journey,' Helen acknowledged. 'Buddy is the most beautiful, shiny, alert dog and he loves you and you love him. We can see that connection and you've done an amazing job.'

The judges had noticed Buddy's fresh face and personality

and could sense he knew how much Zoe loved him. There were moments in the finale when Buddy stood proud and that only came with having a very special relationship – and one that set him and Zoe apart from the others. He also had just a bit more of an edge to his focus on the livestock.

Cilla let rip with an enthusiastic 'Yeowwww' and buried Zoe in a hug. Everyone's smiles were genuine. There were no losers here.

'He's her Buddy,' Neil called out.

'He's my Buddy,' Zoe repeated quietly, giving her champion dog another rub.

Watching Zoe standing there, surrounded by the other participants, with Frank's yards and all the dogs around her, I could imagine the moments – good and bad – of the past year flashing before her eyes. I wondered what that tight camera shot focused on her face would reveal in the edit room. She had feared at one point that she wouldn't even be able to keep Buddy alive, given how sick he'd been, let alone help him become a champion. When I'd spoken to her over the months, she'd felt so doubtful about her own place in the industry that she'd contemplated selling her dogs and leaving, maybe even moving overseas and doing something entirely different.

There was one person in the group who understood the enormity of the announcement more than anyone, and that was Frank. And he had some advice for the woman 45 years his junior. 'Take the opportunity in both hands and represent the industry and showcase the kindness to dogs and be nice to people and you can't go wrong,' he told her warmly.

Later that night, as we all gathered at the pub in town for an end-of-shoot dinner, Zoe confessed that she had been feeling a bit lost during some of our conversations over the previous months. But she already seemed energised by the results. 'Now I plan to run a team of about eight dogs and continue educating weaners. I've already been booked for jobs in the Northern Territory,' she declared happily.

I asked if she felt ready for the publicity once the program aired. Frank had told me Annie had travelled 28,000 kilometres after being named the first champion Muster Dog and he was already fielding invitations for the next champion and their trainer to join him for appearances at country shows.

'You've just got to get ready,' Zoe told me confidently.

It was a big crowd that night, filling the long wooden tables out the back of the pub. The young staff weaved around us all, trying to find the owners of the barramundi or the rump steak. The participants and their extended families were there, and plenty of locals who'd contributed to the success of the week. Members of the Country Women's Association, who'd catered for the 30 cast and crew on the farm, sat conspiratorially at the end of one table, delighting in asking people which sandwiches we'd preferred each day. I confessed I'd only had one day to enjoy their food, but it had been a tasty ham, cheese and tomato. I got the impression I'd

A dozen cameras and drones were used for the announcement of the
champion Muster Dog. (Jesse Smith)

And the winners are ... Zoe and Buddy. (Jesse Smith)

stumbled into a friendly competition with the maker of the egg and lettuce sandwiches and left them to their discussions.

The local mayor offered a thoughtful speech about the role *Muster Dogs* had played in connecting city and country. And Frank, who would always be remembered for his kindness to 'lovely dogs', brought us to tears as he spoke. We knew Frank's family had faced some difficult moments over the past year, and there in that room among friends, with the cameras off, he let his guard down.

There could be no public announcement of Buddy and Zoe's news that night. No cheers from the crowd for the dog that had excelled. The program wouldn't air for another six months, and although everyone at the pub had supported the participants in some way, many still weren't privy to the secret of who had won, and the producers wanted to keep it that way. Zoe's parents had been told earlier that day. They arrived at the pub with her 92-year-old grandad, who was so proud but worried that at his age he'd forget it was a secret and spoil the surprise. With a touch of melancholy, he told me that his goal now was to be alive to see the program go to air.

Lily, who'd done a terrific job with Snow, was more relaxed than I'd ever seen her. She had never grown comfortable in the spotlight and admitted she was utterly relieved it wasn't Snow's name that Helen had called out.

I spotted Cilla in the corner, wrangling her kids as they wrapped their tiny hands around pizzas, threatening to smear her with sauce. She felt so proud of Ash and had been thinking about her own personal journey. 'I've understood the negative parts of my personality that I've always struggled with, that came to the surface because I'd been put under so much pressure with this show and wanting to give Ash every chance to become a champ. But I learned new skills to deal with it all,' she told me, clearly pleased that she'd managed to juggle everything. 'I've had to work on myself as much as I've had to work on Ash.'

Cilla wasn't the only one. As they said their goodbyes that night, there was a combined sense of contentment in the group, a sense of a job well done. And it was clear friends had been made.

*

The next morning most of the others were gone before I'd even woken up. Utes, dogs and kids had been packed up early for their journeys home. I stayed on for another day to take advantage of the beautiful scenery and capture a photo for the front of this book.

The photographer, Jesse Smith, had set up high on a hilltop with the undulating landscape of central Queensland behind me, a large piece of heavy-duty fabric blocking the sun just enough to provide the perfect light for our shoot. Monica convinced Neil, Helen, Mick and Carolyn to rustle up some dogs and join us for the photo. Zoe and Buddy were still in town so they came along with Frank to watch. I looked out at that group and thought about what a privilege it had been to spend time with them, to witness the respect they have for their animals and the land they work.

Helen handed me a wriggling, energetic kelpie puppy and warned, 'Don't let go because he doesn't have any recall yet.' Imagining him taking off over the paddocks, I gripped him tightly as I balanced on three bales of hay while Australia's best dog trainers whistled and cajoled their animals to sit next to me. Jesse told me to 'just keep smiling and looking at the camera – ignore the dogs'. So I smiled, and smiled, and Jesse snapped hundreds of photos in quick succession as the dogs leapt on and off me, falling down and jumping back up, barking with joy, and licking my neck so ardently they threatened to topple me off the bales.

The next day Neil helped Helen pack up one of their trucks and the ute – and all the sheep and goats and dogs – and waved goodbye as she retraced their path back to South Australia with their friend John. The bulls had been left at a saleyard on the jinxed journey up to Queensland so at least they didn't have them to worry about. Neil was heading two hours southwest to hold one of his dog schools. Zoe had already signed up. She left a few hours after the photoshoot and was going to stay in Toowoomba to help her mum and dad on their property before attending the dog school. Buddy might have become a champion, but his young owner felt like she still had a lot to learn.

Mick and Carolyn headed back to their property near Dubbo. Mick had to start preparing for the next dog show, where he'd compete in his beloved sheep trials, the competitions that had made him a national champion.

And Frank would continue doing what he loved – working with his muster dogs and reminding people that kindness was the answer to almost everything.

Buddy overcame sickness to become the champion of series two. (Ben Emery)

CHAPTER 8

Frank to the Rescue

We started this *Muster Dogs* experiment with an overarching question: is it nature or nurture that creates a champion working dog? Is it the genetic traits or the training?

It turns out the answer is … both.

'Good dogs are bred, and champions are made.' That's the voice of experience speaking: Neil McDonald, our trainer, guiding light, steady advisor and judge. 'If you want a champion muster dog, you need both elements at a high level,' he says. Helen McDonald reckons you could easily have a brilliant dog that ends up on the wrong side of the tracks; because they are so intelligent, they can quickly learn how to cheat the system and become impossible to handle.

Neil illustrates this idea by recounting a salutary tale of Colin Creed, a talented young police officer in South Australia in the late 1960s. Creed was dux of his intake class and his intellectual prowess saw him quickly rise through the ranks. But he turned to crime and became one of Australia's most wanted before ending up in jail.

It might seem odd to compare a human with an animal, but Neil says the link is the brilliance. 'You can't have a brilliantly bred dog that isn't trained properly. You've got to have a good dog with good work traits that's also intelligent and can think on its feet under pressure.'

That perfectly sums up our Muster Dogs. All of them – even Lucifer, with extra guidance from Frank – were able to deliver the goods.

But what happens if your dog is proving almost impossible to train? It doesn't matter if you're on a farm or in the suburbs, it's equally frustrating. Neil and Helen say they have been asked for help by owners of 'delinquents of the city obedience groups', so if you're having trouble with your own dog, you're not alone. 'One of the problems we've seen is that people don't discipline a dog until they've done their block with it – and that's too late,' Neil tells me.

'Dog owners need to set boundaries, whether it's in the backyard or the home. You tell them, "You can go here, but you can't cross this line." Or, "You can't jump on that couch because that's where everyone else sits. This is yours back there,"' Helen says, pointing her arm to the back of the loungeroom to suggest where she'd send a dog.

But what happens if everything you've tried doesn't work? I knew who else to ask.

*

Frank Finger and his wife, Cathy, had just finished their breakfast coffees – white, no sugar – when a car they didn't recognise came up their driveway. It was around 7am, the morning after the first episode of *Muster Dogs* series one had aired, and the phone had been busy with excited friends ringing. Two strangers hopped out of the car to congratulate Frank on the show – oh, and by the way they needed help with their kelpie. In fact, they wondered coyly, would Frank be interested in mating their dog with one of his?

As Frank tells me this story, he has a laugh and says, 'I could have brought out a fox terrier and they would have been happy.'

The requests for help haven't stopped, but Frank treats each question with a patience that makes you think he's hearing it for the first time.

Why won't my dog listen to me? Why does my dog misbehave on the lead? Why is my dog barking so much? And then the question that stumps him: Why can't my dog be like Annie?

It isn't just people on the land. City folk also pepper him with their frustrations.

Why won't my dog come to me when I call it? How do you stop a dog incessantly barking? My dog wants to stop and wee all the time while we walk – should I curb this?

The gentle central Queensland grazier doesn't consider himself an expert, but he's learned a thing or two over the last four decades. That knowledge goes back to the first dog he owned. Benno was a black and tan kelpie with long straight legs. 'He was proud of himself. I reckon when he walked and there was a shadow, he'd be sneaking a glance at how good his shadow looked,' Frank says, reminiscing with a smile in his voice. 'He was like a pure-bred racehorse strutting around after a win.'

Benno was the kind of dog that even took pride in his kennel. 'It was so clean you could eat your lunch off it,' Frank recalls. 'Even if he was muddy-footed – next morning, it would be clean. I suppose he did it with his tail or whatever.'

He'd bought Benno and Benno's brother from a breeder who wasn't convinced she'd made the right choice of dogs to mate. The two of them were chalk and cheese. 'One did all the pretty work, and one did the hard work,' Frank says. Benno was the unstoppable hard worker. 'Even in the early days, when our cattle weren't that good to control, he could lock them up and do all the logistical things.'

Benno was almost a year old when Frank made what could have been a fatal mistake. 'Being inexperienced, I'd done something I should never have done,' he tells me. 'We were going to muster another property, rough country, about twenty-odd kilometres away, and Benno jumped up into the sleeper part of the cabin. We were carting horses and when we got to this place, we got the horses off the truck, and we were riding out into the paddock, and I looked behind and he wasn't there.

'Then I looked way ahead, and I could see cattle on the move. He'd seen the cattle before me and by the time we got there he'd gone even further. I did hear him bark in the distance at one stage. Eventually we found all these cattle in a corner, all nice and steady and standing – he'd rounded them up and we picked them up and took them back to the yard. I thought Benno might circle back to the truck, but he wasn't there.'

Frank and his team had gone out at 8am. At lunchtime they had to move on. There was no sign of the lost dog.

'By the time I'd got home, put the horses away and was putting my other dog away, here's Benno, in his kennel, sitting there with the door open! He'd come all the way home across the busy Clermont–Alpha Road. How did he know where we lived? He was up in the sleeper cab not seeing the road. How would he know? I think about watching all the birds flying to Lake Eyre when it's full, and when things like this happen, I think dogs are the same.'

Frank was so mystified he tried to retrace Benno's steps the next day but couldn't find any tracks along the road. 'I think he came a direct route through that range country.'

Benno was that kind of dog. He worked so hard he got sore-footed, and Frank made little boots for him and left him at home to rest his paws. But not much stopped that dog.

'Someone must have opened a gate, the house gate, and let him out. We were eight or nine kilometres away, coming in with the cattle, and he'd turn up there with his little boots on, hobbling away. We had ten different ways we could have come in with those cattle. How did he know which way we were coming?'

He was a majestic, beautiful dog, Frank says, and irreplaceable. Owning Benno, and then losing Benno when he died of old age, taught Frank something very important. You can't keep looking for a perfect dog. 'I fell into the trap of trying to replace him, and then I learned over time that rather than looking for a special dog, you need to just get a pup and make him special.'

If anyone can help with some of the questions *Muster Dogs* viewers have asked about their own dogs, it's Frank. So I call him up on a Tuesday morning at 7am and warn him he could be in for a long chat. He seems almost gleeful about the challenge and tells me to start firing off viewers' queries. We'll do this the way I'd do a Q and A on TV. But stand by, because in reality this is Frank giving me a masterclass.

'Okay, Frank,' I start, 'can dogs sense your emotions? Do they know when things aren't right?'

ABC
ER DOGS
IGER & ANNIE

Rob Tuncks and Frank Finger and their dogs Lucifer and Annie were stars at the 2022 Casterton Kelpie Muster. (Lisa Millar)

Frank: In 2013, I had an accident with a bulldozer. A blade came down on me, broke my pelvis and pushed my hip up through my pelvis. It was the longest I'd been away from my dogs. When I came home from hospital, I had a walking frame. When I went down to let the dogs out, they were all calm. I sat down on a chair, and they kept their distance and then all just sat around me. It's like they knew I was in trouble; they knew something was wrong. And they did that until I got better. If I'm unwell they seem to know, they seem to be concerned for me and behave better than normal. When I'm bright and chirpy, so are they.

Lisa: Do you communicate with all your dogs in the same way?

Frank: I give them all kindness and care. If, for some reason, you don't like a pup or a dog – if you've got a hang-up over something, and you just can't make yourself like it – give it to someone else. It can be their pride and joy. I rarely have that issue now, but I used to after I lost Benno because I was always trying to replace him. It's why I always buy a pup and not a dog. I can make a pup into a special dog.

Lisa: Can you spoil a dog?

Frank: You can. I think probably the worst thing is to overfeed and fuss too much. There's a difference between a house pet and a working dog. But I see handlers blame problems on full moons or bad cows when they've actually spoilt the dog. Dogs need to have boundaries and learn what to do and what not to do. When we open the kennel to let them out in the morning or let them off the chain they've got to be sitting still, not trying to bounce up and down on the chain or bounce out through the door. When we open the door, the dog stays in there until you tell it to hop down. If you don't set those boundaries that is spoiling a dog. It'll push over you and jump up on you. It wants to invade your space and you can't have that. It's all right to call them in for a bit of a cuddle and smooch, but you don't want them jumping over you.

Lisa: How do you stop a dog jumping up on you?

Frank: When it's a very little pup, you sit down and you have it on a lead so you can pull it in towards you a little bit, and there's pressure on the lead. And if they come flying in, you just give them a little smack on the nose, just with the back of your hand. Or you could use something like a plastic cricket bat, something that makes a hollow noise, and just give them a little tap with that. And they stay 30 centimetres away in that comfort zone and then you reach out and give them a pat. And they have to stay there till you give them some sort of cue to call them in. I know some people who've had house dogs – they've had to give them away when they [the owners] got too old because the dogs knocked them over. You shouldn't let that happen in the first place.

Lisa: You're making it sound simple, but tell me more about how you do it.

Frank: They learn to not do things. You tell them to jump up on a bike or a bale of hay and then they have to stay there. I used to do a little growl like 'Ahhh, ahhh' if they were about to jump down and then I'd say, 'Down'. Neil used to hate the noise I made. He said it sounded like I was an old crow. But I've just started doing something different that I've learned from someone who was visiting and it's working well for me.

When a dog does something undesirable, from the time it's a little pup, I'm now giving a sharp, stern 'NO'. It's all about the tone of voice. The dog associates that with the fact it's doing something wrong.

I'm always open to learning new techniques. But it's important to keep everything small and keep all your commands simple. They don't want a head full of commands. My commands are 'Up', 'Down', and 'Over' and 'Back' when they're working. You can talk to them all day, but don't use the commands they've got to respond to unless you need them to do it. If you give them a command that they know and they don't respond, don't move on until they respond or carry it out.

Lisa: Do you think dogs like to be hugged? I read a book that said they don't like it at all.

Frank: Well, I don't read books about dogs. I've only read one a long time ago. This is all from my experience. I wouldn't call it hugging, but some dogs like being patted and getting close to you. I did have one kelpie that the breeder said to me, 'She's from a line of dogs that don't like a lot of affection.' She would sit right back on the bike away from me. When I'm feeding them and they come in one at a time for a bit of a talk, she would never come near me. Maybe it was a line of dogs that hadn't been treated well and she'd evolved to be suspicious and skittish. Why do dingoes gallop away from us? Because we hunt them. Why do kangaroos hop away as soon as they see us? Because they know about roo shooters. Yet other animals that aren't hunted, like butcher birds, will come in and nearly pinch the bread off your plate.

Lisa: What do you do about that?

Frank: If we get a dog that's hard to catch, we walk up sideways or let the dog come up from behind, because they've worked out that if they come from behind you, you can't do as much damage [in their eyes] as if you are front-on. That's just my thoughts.

Lisa: Are working dog's tails and pet dog's tails different in how they use them?

Frank: The tail has to be down when kelpies are working. With really good kelpies you'll see they've tucked their tail right between their legs and it runs up along their lower stomach. If the tail is up when they're working, it means the brain is not engaged. And, of course, when they're off duty and they're wagging their tail, they're contented and happy. If they're not wagging it, it's time to check its temperature. You must assess your working dogs every morning to check nothing has happened the day before that you've missed and that they need help for.

Lisa: How much sleep do dogs need?

Frank: Working dogs need plenty of sleep and they can go into a deep, deep sleep. When we camp out they're not too far away from us and if you get up in the middle of the night they'll be sound asleep. You can walk right up to them and nearly put your hand on them. They wake up with a start, just like we do. They'll go to sleep as soon as you get somewhere at the end of the day. Or if you stop for a lunch break the dogs will just go to sleep. It's why it's important not to have non-working dogs or other dogs that bark at night because it's like trying to sleep near someone who snores. If I have a dog that's barking, I go down and take it away from the kennel and put it somewhere else until I have taught it not to bark.

Lisa: Why won't a dog come when you call it? And how do you change that?

Frank: They haven't been trained properly. Or you haven't shown them affection when they do come to you. You have to be calling them in the right tone. They say with children, if you're at a picnic or you're somewhere near a waterhole and your child's disappeared and you panic and start calling their name, they'll freeze. A dog does the same because you've panicked and the dog thinks that you're after it. Neil talks about the Five Rs when you call a dog – request, remind, reinforce, response and reward. I would say 'Annie' in a pleasant voice as my request. And then a reminder – 'Annie' – and I will sound a bit sterner and then reinforce that request with an even sterner voice if she still hasn't come. As soon as she does, she gets the reward. 'Lovely dog, lovely dog.' It's all about the tone.

Lisa: But how do you fix it, if they're not coming to you?

Frank: We get people to check their demeanour and just calm down a bit. Just change back a gear. Neil talks about imagining you're having a puff of marijuana, and I think he's right, you've just got to calm down. Sometimes at the dog schools at the end of the day we will bring out a few beers and people have their out-of-school time and then they do the tasks effortlessly because it's just relaxed them a little bit. It's all about

demeanour and it took me a long time to work that out.
Just calm down.

Lisa: What if you've had a pet dog for a couple of years
and it ignores your calls? Can you fix that or have you
lost the battle?

Frank: I don't think there's ever a battle lost. I would
have that dog on a long lead, just a light lead, like a
chainsaw starter cord, about 5 or 6 metres long. Or
maybe use a plastic clothesline that's coated and durable
and put it on a clip. So if you can get the dog to run
away from you or just run around and stand on the end
of the lead, just as it's about to hit the end of the lead,
call its name. And you call it just a split second before it
hits the end of the lead. And then eventually, as soon as
you call its name, it's waiting for the lead to yank, so it'll
turn around and come to you.

We have long leads on our little pups all the time.
You never want a situation where you've let your little
pup out and for some reason it starts to dodge you and
it knows that you're going to put it away. And that's
the next little trick. If you tie your dogs up or put them
away, catch them a couple of times first. Don't just catch
it when you're going to put it away because it knows
that you're putting it away. When you've got it out and
having a bit of fun, just catch it and give it a little pat.
And then next time, just catch it and put it away. So

don't only call your dog when you want to put it away
or do something that it doesn't like.

Lisa: Are working dogs 'wired' for one owner or can
someone else give them instructions?

Frank: My son, Scott, and I work together all the time.
If it was desperate, I could probably borrow one of his
and he'd borrow one of mine. But it's not wise because
they can go looking for him or they come looking for
me.

Lisa: Are dogs allowed in your house?

Frank: Our dogs aren't allowed in the house. We might
have them in the laundry or on the veranda if they're
crook or you're worried about them. I think Annie might
have walked through the house a couple of times. Annie
has a few privileges, but the rest of the team don't see it.

Lisa: What's some of the oddest behaviour you've seen in
a dog?

Frank: Well, funnily enough, Annie won't eat while I'm
looking at her. I don't know why. I'll put fresh steak in
her kennel and she'll just stare at it. And then I go away
and come back a few minutes later and it's all gone.

Lisa: On the show, you once described sniffing as
unsociable. I thought all dogs sniffed. What's wrong
with that?

Frank: They do, but they don't have to. A lot of working
dogs fight and that comes from the peeing on things,

marking their territory. That's their territory. He's the boss. Well, on my farm, I'm the boss wolf. All the dogs are equal and they've got to ask me where they can pee. Neil McDonald is probably the best I've ever seen for control over dogs. He lets all his dogs go out in the morning, and there could be 15, there could be 20, and they all empty out without cocking their leg. They go way away, empty it, do their business, and come back all fresh-faced to him. And if they sniff, he gives them a bit of a tap. Annie is probably one of the worst I've had for wanting to sniff all the time. Their attention should be on you or on the livestock. Sniffing is a distraction. And marking the territory just starts fights. Dogs must not fight. My dogs can't fight with me, and they can't fight with each other.

Lisa: But what if the dogs need to wee some more?

Frank: If you're letting it out early in the morning and late in the afternoon, they should have completely clean kennels. If not, you're doing something wrong. They take pride in their kennel and they don't dirty in their kennels and they wait.

Lisa: What advice do you have for people in the city training their pups?

Frank: I think that to get complete control, if I was in a suburban area, I would build a kennel or I would have some sort of freight box or plastic crate. Because dogs are a cave animal and they like that enclosure, you want to give pups that environment. I would have those little plastic crates. Put the pup in that at night and get it used to that. And you can have it in the laundry if you want, so you can keep a check on it. And if it barks, just go down and hit the ground with a rake or a broom. Rattle their cage. You've always got to have a home for them. Have a chain or a kennel. Don't let dogs off, even pet dogs, 24 hours a day because they run up and down the front fence, waiting for the mailman to come. Then they start biting. All those bad habits and behaviours are all learned.

Lisa: You're not keen on hearing dogs barking, are you?

Frank: I couldn't live in town. For God's sake, your dogs are barking! There's no need for dogs to bark. If a dog barks, there's something wrong in the family setup. It's lonely. It's bored. There's something wrong or it's just become a habit. Stop it. It's all right if there's a reason, if it's letting you know it's out of water or something. But if I hear a dog barking, I know it's stressed. I don't want to go and flog the dog. I just want to go and get it and take it to a better spot. It's like Luci [formerly known as Lucifer], you'd never hear from him, but the moment you put him in the back of a ute, he barks. And I go around, and I say, 'What's wrong, buddy?' And I don't think he knows, but he just barks. And I remember one time we went to a dog school at Isisford and my daughter Julie bought a dog off someone. And on the way home, every time we'd go over a cattle grid, the dog would bark. Hit the grid, dog barks. Hit the grid, dog barks. Well, we just had to stop that before it became a lifelong habit because there are a lot of grids! We had a towel hanging over the cage so he couldn't see out and if he couldn't see the grid he didn't bark.

Lisa: It takes a lot of work, it seems, to fix these problems.

Frank: When you get your little puppy, you've got to be committed to see it through. No excuses, otherwise you'll have six months of excuses or you'll have six months of progress. I liken it to a jigsaw puzzle. If you went out and bought a jigsaw puzzle with 365 pieces and you put one piece in the right spot every day, at the end of the year, you would have a puzzle worth looking at. If you bought that same puzzle, mixed it all up, threw it in a shopping bag and threw it in the kennel and shut the door and then went out and got it 12 months later you're going to have a jumbled mess. You need to do one little thing every day.

Lisa: If your dog is misbehaving, should you ever just wait to see if it'll grow out of it?

Frank: Look, things do pass, but don't let it become a habit. Don't laugh at it or make an excuse. Just try to fix it.

Lisa: Do you punish puppies?

Frank: Just little bits of discipline all the way. If you've got an older dog you have to be a bit more visible with your discipline. To get the bluetooth going on an older dog, we have them on a lead where we can give a couple of little sharp jerks when they're not looking at you or when they run past you. The dog should walk beside you. When it goes past you, give it a little snap on the lead and that's how you get it to come back and stay with you.

Lisa: Do you think routines are good for dogs?

Frank: I probably do because every morning I let them out for a run. Same in the afternoon. I sit on the chair and they all come in one by one for a little talk with me. It gives me a chance to assess them. If one fella carries his hind leg, he might have got hurt the day before. If one's a bit wonky, I'll do a check with my thermometer. Scott, my son, did a check the other day on one of his dogs and it was 41.9 and the vet said come straight in and she put him on the drip and saved his life. If we'd taken him out to work, he'd have been dead. You just have to watch them all the time.

Lisa: Do dogs sulk?

Frank: I don't think so. I've seen plenty of sulking from the handlers, but I don't think I've ever seen dogs sulk.

Lisa: Can one dog cause chaos in a team?

Frank: One dog can teach the other dogs to bark. One

dog can teach your dogs to howl. And we have a little bit of trouble in April every year because that's mating season for the dingoes. And the male dingoes howling in the distance, perhaps up to 3 kilometres away, can start the working dogs in their kennels howling as well. If I hear a dog howling, I'll bounce out of bed, I will crack a whip and make a noise. You've got to nip that in the bud.

Lisa: Can dogs have 'off' days?

Frank: Yes, and you'll see that when you let them out of the kennel. They mightn't go to eat at night, or they just mightn't be as chirpy in the morning. And once again you check the temperature. If that's all right, just leave that dog at home. I don't think they're any different to humans. And if you think, *I shouldn't take that dog, but I'll take him anyway*, it normally ends in grief, so go with your gut feeling.

Lisa: Can dogs have anxiety?

Frank: Probably not, although they don't like loud noises. When I'm taking Luci and Annie to shows, I have to get them well away before the fireworks. We got caught at the Emerald Show – we'd just come off after doing our little thing and before we could get them to the car the fireworks started, and if I didn't have them on a lead, I'd have lost both of them. The committee made a path for us to get out of there, and back at the motel they didn't stop trembling for three hours.

*

The bond between Frank and Annie was immediate and not much has changed. Frank has always argued against having a favourite on the farm, but he had to break his own rule with Annie, who goes everywhere with him.

'She sits up in the back of the twin cab in the air conditioning,' he says. It's the least he can do, given what he asks of her. She's been the star attraction at hundreds of media and community shows around Australia, including at the Casterton Kelpie Muster, which is held every year in the town considered the birthplace of kelpies. That's where I met Annie for the first time and even managed to pick her up for a quick cuddle before she wriggled her way out of my grasp. There's only one person Annie is interested in and that's Frank. And the feelings are mutual.

Not all their trips are easy – in particular, a visit to Tasmania for the Bream Creek Show, about a 45-minute drive east of Hobart, was testing for both of them. The company overseeing Annie's travel requires three and a half hours between connecting flights to make sure she's properly boarded into the cargo hold. But on the way to Tassie, the connection at Brisbane was too tight. Annie missed her flight and had to stay overnight in Brisbane.

Frank picked her up at the airport in Hobart the following afternoon and wasn't happy that they'd been separated. He thinks the rules should be that animals always travel on the same plane as their owners. An airline staff member reassured him that Annie had been looked after. She had food and water, and a vet had been on hand.

'And I said to her, "What about the human welfare thing, because that's been the longest time I've ever been away from Annie!"'

Frank's not the only one who worries about Annie's health and wellbeing. Annie's vet, Tess Salmond, has been contemplating getting cotton wool earplugs for Annie to reduce the stress that comes with her centre-stage appearances around Australia. Dr Tess, as she's known to locals in Clermont, has been caring for Frank's animals since she started working alongside her veterinary father, Alan, who set up the surgery in the mid-1970s. But she's never had a patient as famous as Annie.

'I didn't really cotton on at the beginning because I'm not a very suspicious person,' she told me, relaying what happened when Frank brought Annie in as a pup for her first shots. 'He said, "Oh, do you mind if we film this?" and I think, *Cripes, this is escalating.* And then Frank said, "We're doing a thing," but of course it was all secret.' Besides, it wasn't the first time she'd been asked to film a procedure; her cousin was a principal at a remote school in Barcaldine and she'd filmed a puppy being vaccinated so he could share it with the Grade Ones.

'I didn't really understand the significance of it till I watched *Muster Dogs.* The company that owns the surgery now is a big company and the big kahuna who lives in the city messaged me and he's like, "Oh my god, Frank from Clermont has won *Muster Dogs* – do you know him??"'

As Tess told me how much it meant for the community to see the public outpouring of love for Frank, she started to tear up. 'They're not Instagramming or influencing or anything like that; they're just genuine souls of the earth, beautiful people doing so much for rural Australia.'

Tess is also an amazing example of the sometimes-unsung heroes of life in the deepest and remotest parts of Australia. She's part of the chain of support that helps keep the show on the road for the region's graziers and their communities.

When I spoke to her, it was nine o'clock on a Sunday morning and she'd been up most of the previous night. A French bulldog had been bitten by a brown snake and its frantic owner had brought her to the vet surgery late in the evening.

'It's a tragic case because the beautiful older lady had two dogs and one had been found dead at lunchtime next to the big snake,' she told me. 'I met her in the driveway and gave her a big hug and carried this little body inside and the lady was just sobbing and it ripped my heart out. But we thought her other dog, his sister, was okay. But then after dinner she just started bleeding everywhere from her mouth, from her nose, and by the time they got here the little dog's tongue was blue and she was choking.'

It's the reality of bush practices that Tess lives next door to the surgery. She was able to immediately put the dog, Gloria, on oxygen and administer anti-venom. She also gave her a plasma transfusion and an opioid to calm her. All the time Tess was thinking, *I can't let this dog die. I have to save this dog for my client.*

Leaving a camera set up to monitor the dog, Tess was able to duck home to catch short naps after midnight. Her husband, John, was away that weekend, working on their property four hours north and she was looking after their two young children as well as the clinic and the emergency cases.

'Oh god, Tess, what a night! Is the dog going to live?' I asked, feeling bad that our scheduled chat had coincided with such a rough 12 hours for her.

'I think she's through the worst of it,' she reassured me. 'We've got a few in our little hospital – a big dog with heartworm who's on a drip, and a couple of horses. One of the horses, the poor thing, has swamp cancer. It's a fungal infection, but it looks like a tumour.'

One of her nurses, Lani, had turned up that morning and taken her to task for not calling her in as the patient list grew the night before. She'd entered an event at the annual rodeo and Tess hadn't wanted to ruin her evening. But Lani would have forfeited the competition in a heartbeat to help Tess. In the end another nurse, Trina, had come in unannounced. 'She got wind of the sick little dog because her mum had been friends with the lady who owned the dog. It sums up this community.'

On top of all this, Tess has the added responsibility of caring for Annie, a household name in the working dog world thanks to her *Muster Dogs* win. The prize kelpie is travelling so often, to so many different parts of Australia, that Tess dedicates a lot of thought to making sure Annie's vaccinated against whatever threat might arise.

'We're in a heartworm area here, so she's on that,' Tess explained. 'Then if, for example, Frank's taking her to the Atherton Show, there's the risk of leptospirosis, which is bacteria in the water, and then also paralysis ticks. So wherever she's going, we need to address the health concerns.' Tess also works with Frank to minimise the stress for Annie of suddenly being a frequent flyer. 'She's a high-performance athlete, you know.'

One thing hasn't changed: in all the time she's known Frank she's marvelled at his approach with animals. 'He'll ring me and he'll say, "Tess, Annie's not right." He'll just pick something up. And it's so subtle, but he's just such an animal person. He's just got that sixth sense.'

But even Tess was amazed to learn Frank had taken on an added challenge in series two of *Muster Dogs*: training Lucky, the deaf dog from the litter of border collie pups. Frank himself was unsure how it would go. 'Because I talk a lot of blabber to dogs in a nice, soft voice and even sing to them a little bit or do something just to make them settle,' he said. 'And I couldn't do that with him. So I just gave him big cuddles and picked him up and carried him and acted a fool with him so he never got afraid of me.'

When Lucky first arrived at Frank's place, he was a noisy pup who barked through the night. 'When the sun went down, he'd start barking and he wouldn't stop until the sun came up. I wasn't sure what to do the first night, so I turned up the air conditioner and put earplugs in.'

The next day Frank ran a power lead down to the kennel, about 150 metres away from his bedroom. He attached a bright light to a chair and then as soon as Lucky started barking, Frank flicked the light on. 'And he stopped. I turned the light off in the morning. The next night I put the light on again before he started to bark. No barking. And then the third night, I woke up through the night and I thought, *Oh, I didn't turn the light on*, but Lucky wasn't barking. And he hasn't barked since.'

He wonders if Lucky was afraid of the dark. Or if, with the bright light in his little face, he didn't know if Frank or someone else was there behind it. 'Or maybe the light disturbed him and he didn't want it on so he kept quiet. But the point is that anything like barking, or any habit like chasing cars, or chasing the mailman, anything that's an undesirable habit is just that. It's a habit and you've got to break it, in a nice humane way.'

Frank's verbal commands weren't going to work with Lucky. 'I used body language instead, different ways with the rake or how I'd bend over when I wanted him to come to me.'

But first he had to get Lucky's attention. And if you can't call out to a dog, what do you do? That's how Flo, Lucky's girlfriend, got involved. 'I'd just call another dog who was nearby and when the other dog started moving, Lucky looks up,' he explains. 'And if he's looking at me, I then clap my hands or do something, and he'll be there in a cloud of white fur.'

There was the added consideration that Lucky couldn't hear traffic or moving machinery so Frank would have to keep an extra keen watch over him. But he was quickly becoming an alert young dog, simply by watching the others in the team. Their bond was close, almost too close. 'He's like that dog that wants to knock me over, but I've got to let him come in for a big jump and a big fuss. I need that to get him out of trouble. I can't call him. I've got to have him just come at me a million miles an hour. It's going to be a little different.'

Muster Dogs is an experiment on so many levels and Frank's relationship with Lucky is perhaps one of the most challenging of them all. But Frank has proved again that innovation, training and kindness can work its magic in even the most difficult of situations.

CHAPTER 9

Muster Mania

'It's like *The Wiggles* for Doggos!'

And so began the social media deluge after the very first episode of *Muster Dogs* series one. It was just a hint of what was to come. Clea had posted that message. Another viewer, Carol, added: 'My whippet, Sydney, had his eyes glued to the TV for the whole program.'

We knew that *Muster Dogs* would appeal to animal lovers. But we hadn't anticipated how big the dog audience would be. They settled in with their owners to watch their canine cousins – Gossip, Spice, Lucifer, Chet and Annie – do their thing. One viewer confessed she was using *Muster Dogs* as a companion for her pooch, setting it to play the full four hours of the first series while she was at work.

My own Facebook and Instagram feed was flooded with videos of people's dogs, wagging tails in front of the TV or chasing them till they were dizzy. Sometimes the clips showed dogs barking (barking) so loudly while the show was on that any hope their humans had of being able to watch in peace was dashed as their own pets became the night's entertainment. Many wanted to share their own tales of the loyalty and bravery of their working dogs – or just plain naughtiness. Here are just a few.

*

Nina told us about her old dog, Rex, a kelpie blue heeler cross. On one occasion when Nina's dad was visiting, he insisted on keeping his walking shoes at the front door – with his socks tucked inside, of course. Rex couldn't resist taking the socks out to play and Nina's dad, a retired headmaster, decided to train Rex not to take the socks.

'Then came the day Dad triumphantly declared he had finally trained Rex to leave his socks alone,' Nina wrote. 'And at exactly the same time we could see Rex in the background parading Dad's socks, looking very pleased with himself.'

Nina's dad might not have had success with the socks that visit, but he did manage to teach Rex to shake hands. When he returned nearly a year later, he was very moved to find that the first thing Rex did was to greet him by shaking hands.

*

Brisbane resident Ros told us it was an 'absolute joy to vicariously share in the pups' journey' because it brought back fond memories of her childhood on a beef and dairy farm in the New South Wales Northern Rivers region.

Knowing that her dad, Martin, who was 93, could relive his farming days and remember the 15 working dogs he'd had through his lifetime made it even more special.

'My dad's respect for, and connection to, his dogs was always the sweetest thing to witness,' she wrote. 'They were always most content together, whether it was out in the paddock rounding up cows or sitting on the patio in the sun, dog underfoot, listening to the radio. Like Frank on the show, Dad would constantly talk with his dogs and tell them how lovely they were. He even managed to forgive one particularly energetic dog, Milly, whose excited actions caused Dad to fall and crack his sternum and end up in hospital for four months!'

Ros's dad died a year after the first series went to air. She says his lively dog Milly still waits for his return. 'If there are dogs in heaven, I'm sure my dad will be surrounded by several right now.'

*

Another viewer, Karina, told us her dog, Alfie, was a 16-year-old 'westie poo', which is a cross between a West Highland terrier and a poodle. And he was as deaf as a post. 'He would sleep with one eye open so he could see when *Muster Dogs* began,' Karina told me. At the first sight of the dogs, he'd be up dancing a jig like a puppy with his ears flapping. His bones no longer weary, he'd be barking with all the glee of a youngster.

*

Ten-year-old kelpies Tilly and Lexi curled up on a swag to watch the series with their humans and four other canine friends. The dogs' ears pricked up when they heard the whistles coming from the TV. Tilly and Lexi's owner, Chris, said she and her friend Georgie laughed and cried throughout the four episodes – hoping the pups would all pass each milestone.

Chris was taken with how relatable and believable the show was. 'I know first and foremost what it's like to have a "failed" kelpie as a working dog,' she told me, admitting that both Tilly and Lexi would fall into that category.

Tilly and Lexi were a couple of 'city princesses' who lived in Sydney but got to experience country life on a Merino sheep farm in rural Mudgee in New South Wales. On the car journey to Mudgee, for the first three and a half hours, the two kelpies would be quiet and peaceful. But once they left the city, their noses would start to twitch and Lexi would cry with excitement knowing where she was headed.

The kelpie instinct was dominant in both of them, and they would quickly shed their city habits and start with their daily jobs: rounding up any sheep swimming in the creek, watching the kangaroos hop on by. They'd roll in anything that smelled rotten, wearing it like a badge of honour.

Lexi came from a working property north of Newcastle and there were great expectations of her. Her breeding line was good. Her father had the bloodline and was a 'Prince' and her mum was 95 per cent kelpie. 'From a young pup, she started to show some unusual behaviours,' Chris said. 'She hated the car and would hyperventilate, not engage, not listen, become anxious. She'd run in the other direction trying to herd anything bigger than herself. All these traits were not what I expected, so instead of becoming a working dog she became a lap dog.' Lexi was known as 'Doona' in the house because she could be found on the bed given any opportunity.

Tilly was the matriarch of the pack. All the other dogs respected her and looked up to her. She was the quiet achiever who always stayed close to Chris. 'As a pup she had a rough life when she found herself in the wrong hands and was kicked, abused and chained up. By the time we got her, her neck was lacerated, swollen and infected from the chain. Trust was a big thing. She was never going to be a working dog. Training, trust and love was what she needed.' As a result,

Tilly has become a wonderful dog – loyal, calm and able to read situations around her. 'When we're at the farm you can always find Tilly lying on the front porch. She has made it her job to ensure she always puts herself between the outside and the inside. She has supported my mental health and is instinctive beyond words. She is my best friend. She knows when to sit by your side or give you a gentle nuzzle to say, "I'm here for you."'

Chris sometimes took Tilly and Lexi to the local nursing home, where they'd delight the elderly residents, particularly those with farming backgrounds. 'Their eyes light up and they come to life telling you about their childhoods and their dogs.'

For Chris, *Muster Dogs* confirmed that not all kelpies are made to work or pass the criteria. For whatever reason, some just don't make the cut, but they can still be the most amazing and rewarding breed of dog to have. 'Tilly and Lexi are the best versions of failed working dogs and what they can still deliver and achieve. You can take the dog out of the country, but you can't take the country out of the dog.'

*

The program proved to be a problem solver for another two viewers. Kathleen and her husband had moved from a townhouse in suburban Brisbane to Bannockburn, half an hour west of Geelong in Victoria, for a new life in the country.

Their cat, Jett, came with them. She had been adopted from a shelter and was most definitely a house cat – in fact she'd never been allowed outside. When she was introduced to her new country home, she was put on a leash and allowed to happily explore the chook pen and the veggie patch. She was not as relaxed, however, around the other long-term resident, a kelpie called Lulu.

Lulu loved other animals and expected Jett to be a new friend, Kathleen told us, but Jett was highly suspicious and stayed well clear. Kathleen settled onto her bed one night to watch *Muster Dogs* with Jett snuggled up beside her. As each puppy came on the screen, Kathleen would pat Jett and say, 'Yes, that's another Lulu, and look, there's another Lulu.' Jett moved closer and closer to the screen, tilting her head in wonder at these 'other Lulus'.

Jett may have been a cat, but Kathleen was convinced she was taking in what she was seeing on the screen. The more they watched the show together, the more Jett seemed to connect it to how Lulu acted around her. Jett seemed to relax into a newfound comfort of knowing Lulu wasn't a threat and they developed a strong friendship. 'It's sweet to watch and it's all because of *Muster Dogs*. Jett is so much calmer now, and Lulu will come to the kitchen door in the morning with a bark to say, "Come on out and play," and she does!'

Kathleen has had a long appreciation for working dogs. She said it was always a treat as a kid to visit her grandmother in

Casterton in Victoria, the home of the annual Kelpie Muster. 'It is just so good for everyone to understand a little bit more about how the working dogs have contributed to farming life in Australia.'

*

There's nowhere quite like the Casterton Kelpie Muster to get a glimpse of just how fanatical people can be about their dogs. There are kelpie statues in the street, and T-shirts for sale covered with dogs. Need a pair of silver kelpie earrings? A tattoo of a kelpie? You can get one here. In 2023, the two-day festival attracted the biggest crowds yet: 10,000 visitors over the weekend, with visitors from the United States, United Kingdom and New Zealand. One group drove thousands of kilometres from northwest Australia to watch the dogs competing in a range of events including a high jump, a hill climb, a dash and a street parade.

Our *Muster Dogs* stars – both the humans and the dogs – are now hot-ticket invitees and are mobbed for selfies. The weekend ends with an auction; in 2023, 4000 people gathered to see the top dog go for $25,000 and the top pup sell for $11,000.

Karen Stephens, who's the president of the Casterton Kelpie Association, says every year more and more 'city slickers' turn up with their working dog pets. 'I love watching them, and how game they are putting their dogs up against the farm animals in the competitions.'

One of those city slickers is Tegan Eagle. She'd grown up in the suburbs of Melbourne in a two-storey brick home with her parents, two brothers and a labrador. She'd been desperate to have a kelpie as a pet after visiting friends on a property and witnessing the loyalty this breed exhibited. As she approached the end of high school, her parents relented and Bailey arrived to join the family on their regular-sized suburban block.

'Straight away he was more energetic [than the family's labrador], and I knew that was going to be the case, but he was a lot more loyal and more in tune to me,' she told me. 'You'd take our labrador for a walk to the oval and she'd go to the local school and go sniffing for food scraps and not come back for an hour whereas Bailey would always be more focused on what I was doing.'

There was no formal training. It's not as if Bailey was required to get to work to muster any livestock. He was just a city pet who was showered with love. Not long after Tegan got Bailey, the family embarked on a road trip to the Casterton Kelpie Muster to see what all the fuss was about.

'I entered him in the triathlon, and he did really well in the sprint and the hill climb, and on his first high jump he did great. Then he ran in the opposite direction and didn't want to do it again.'

Despite this, it'd been fun for 19-year-old Tegan and she returned the next year and entered Bailey in the high jump again.

There were a dozen other competitors, some of them arriving with an air of seriousness usually reserved for an Olympic-level sporting event. Bailey was recovering from surgery after slicing his side open chasing rabbits on a friend's property. He had had the stitches removed four days before the Casterton show.

The tension was palpable as Bailey ran at the jump and cleared 2.55 metres. 'I thought, *What the bloody hell?*' Tegan said, reminiscing about the day her city dog ruled the podium. 'I didn't realise he wanted to jump like that, and I told people maybe it was because he'd been resting for so long with the injury that he had all this energy.'

Casterton was abuzz about the newcomers. Tegan and Bailey returned the following year and he won the high jump again, leaping 2.95 metres and breaking the record. And again the year after that. In 2016 he cleaned up, breaking his own high jump record and winning the 50-metre dash as well. He was so good, the organisers put him and Tegan in the hall of fame and asked them not to compete anymore, to give other people a go. 'He's so full of himself, he loves crowds, he loves being the centre of attention; the more crowds he has the more hyperactive he gets.'

Tegan and Bailey were still living in the suburbs and people often asked her how he coped with not being on a property and being able to run around – and given his amazing high jump skills, they also wanted to know how she kept him in her backyard. She told them she never had a problem because he was always exercised or had company.

Bailey became a star. He was interviewed for news stories on TV and in the papers. He strutted through the foyer of Network Ten in Melbourne as if he owned the place. 'My random backyard dog is now getting all this attention for just jumping over a high jump.'

Tegan eventually left Melbourne and moved to Cobargo, a small town about 400 kilometres south of Sydney. Bailey was her constant companion through her twenties. She eventually came back home to her parents, who'd left the city for a property near Nangana, east of the Dandenong Ranges in Victoria. The one-time city slicker, babysitter and nanny became a stable hand. Meanwhile, Bailey, who was enjoying retirement, had a half-brother called Cooper. They shared a mother – and the same skills; when Tegan returned to Casterton, this time with Cooper eight years after she first took part with Bailey, they walked away winners again.

But no one has yet beaten Bailey's record jump of 2.95 metres.

The dogs might live in the country now but neither will ever break any records as skilled working dogs. 'Bailey has seen sheep and he's been to herding training, but if you call him, he's like "Yeah, I've heard that you've called me, but

I might take my time because I'm busy." Everyone said you can't have kelpies in a backyard because they're crazy and so naughty, but even though they take a bit of effort at the start, they're the best dogs in the world.'

*

People also shared some wonderful love stories with us.

When Rohan sold his farm in the face of drought and frosts, he went to work for a friend, harvesting near Lake Grace in Western Australia. Because he'd moved, the geographical reach of his online dating profile had changed. Kate, who was working for a bank in Narrogin, was an hour and a half away, but distances are relative when you're online dating in outback Australia. She was trawling through one profile picture after another of men who weren't quite right when she came across a photo of a beautiful red working dog. She didn't need to see the bloke who owned it. She swiped right and started messaging with Rohan, the owner. Their first date was at a café – and Tex, the kelpie, was there too. 'I tell Rohan that Tex did the leg work,' Kate told me.

When they visited Kate's family for their first Christmas together, her 99-year-old grandmother, Rachel, leaned in and whispered in her ear: 'Keep this one, because you can tell a good man from the land by how his dog respects him.' Her grandmother had been watching Tex, who wasn't moving from his spot beside Rohan's feet.

Rohan had bought Tex for $100 from a retired farmer in 2015, and as family folklore has it, it was the best $100 he'd ever spent. Tex has been by Rohan's side during family conflict and the brutal seasons that forced him to sell the farm. The day Rohan loaded his last mob of sheep onto a truck, it was as if Tex knew his boss was having a hard time so he worked even harder to help.

Rohan and Kate moved in together and eventually married, although even the wedding had Tex's input. He was supposed to wait with Rohan at the altar, but he had other ideas, circling back to the house to escort the bride out to the paddock to her groom. 'It was like he wanted to give me away,' she said.

When they started trying for a baby, things didn't go to plan. And so began a two-year journey through fertility treatment, miscarriages and pregnancies. 'Tex would know before any test if I was pregnant or not pregnant. When I was eventually pregnant, he would not leave my side. He would sleep by my bed and not let anyone near me.'

And when their baby daughter, Rachel, was born, Tex was besotted. 'I don't need a baby monitor because he sits outside her bedroom window and if she cries, he howls. And the little dogs aren't allowed around the pram. He's not aggressive with them, but they're not allowed near it. The pram is the boundary and he'll quite often lay down beside her.'

Rohan and Kate admit he's not the best sheep dog, but he gets the job done. Tex is getting on in years now and doesn't jump like he used to. He needs to be lifted on and off the back of the ute but they don't mind. And they don't mind that, when he does get up there, he barks until they hit 80 kilometres an hour. Without fail. They still don't know why.

'But he is forever working, always helping as much as he can, and we love him for the fact he is the reason our family is together.'

*

After *Muster Dogs* went to air we got a message from a couple in the city of Launceston, in Tasmania. Tracey and Mark wrote in to say thanks, but their message was tinged with sadness. They'd had a beautiful kelpie called Clem who'd died six months earlier and they'd cried and laughed their way through the program, remembering some of the traits they'd seen in their own pet.

I messaged them to see if they'd be up for a chat about Clem and they readily agreed. He was a city kelpie who loved being a little naughty. People thought Tracey and Mark were a bit mad taking on a kelpie because of the breed's reputation for being so energetic, but they were committed to exercising him morning and night. 'We'd wear him out, and he'd sleep all day on our bed, facing onto the front veranda,' Tracy told me. 'The postie would know if we were home or not – if we weren't home, Clem would barely raise an eyebrow. But if we were at home, he would bark and create quite a commotion. He had zero interest in protecting the house but took his job of protecting us very seriously.'

Clem wasn't easy to control. 'Sometimes he'd sit in the middle of the oval and, if I got within five metres of him, he'd run off again,' Tracey said, on speaker phone in their kitchen. 'I'd have to ring Mark and say, "Can you come and get Clem?"'

'Tracey didn't have a gruff-enough voice,' Mark said, piping in with his own memories. 'I'd give him the tough voice regularly, but he was so forgiving. He'd slink off with his tail between his legs and would come back within a couple of minutes with this look in his eyes that said, "We good now?" and of course we were.'

I could picture these two schoolteachers as they spoke to me from their warm kitchen on a winter's morning. It was a tough conversation and Tracey started to cry as she recounted what happened to Clem. They'd been out walking along the river one morning as they always did – a routine so predictable that Tracey could do it with her eyes closed. She'd throw the ball and Clem would chase it but drop it further away, so she'd have to keep walking to fetch it and toss it again. Clem got distracted by some native hens and chased them into thick reeds by the river. He'd been in and out of those reeds so many times on their morning walks that Tracey wasn't worried.

She waited for him to pop up on the other side of the river, but he didn't. 'It was muddy and sloshy, but I walked down to the bank and couldn't see him.' Tracey followed the track along the river, expecting him to show up beside her any minute. When he still didn't turn up, she called for help. Workmates and neighbours began searching. Someone put a boat in. But it wasn't until later that day that Clem's body was found, 50 metres from where Tracey had been standing. 'I don't know if he drowned or had an episode but that sense of blame, that feeling that I was responsible ...' Her voice faltered as she began to cry. 'So watching *Muster Dogs* was tough but really therapeutic as well.'

*

Another viewer confided to us about his own very special dog called Dan, who was also sadly no longer around. Terry's story began in Chinchilla in Queensland at a country fete. There'd been people selling border collie pups and Terry's young cousins had been playing with them. At the end of the day the pups were still there, unsold, and the sellers handed them over to the kids for free. Before their parents got back to say no, the puppy breeders had cleared out and the families had no choice but to take the dogs home.

The pups were energetic and mischievous. At a birthday party for Terry's aunt, someone accidentally let one of them, a pup called Dan, off his chain. Dan, still only about 12 months old, scooted out to the front paddock and immediately corralled a mob of 20 cows. 'My aunty was saying, "That bloody dog, rounding up those cows again," and I said to her, "Well, if you ever need to get rid of him, I'll make sure he goes to a good home."'

Dan eventually ended up with Terry and, after a bit of training and a lot of bonding, he became a great working dog. 'The first I knew I had something really special, I was riding through a large timbered paddock area, a couple of thousand hectares with plenty of hills, and I had him sitting on my lap on the motorbike and another dog behind me,' Terry told me. Dan started to whinge and complain about being on the bike so Terry let him off. 'And he just lit straight out into the timber and shortly after started barking into the trees.'

Dan had found a mob of cattle and a bullock that had jumped out of the yards a few years before and hadn't been seen since. 'I was so impressed with Dan that he'd just pulled them up on his own.'

A few years on, late in the day, Terry and his brother Sam were driving through a densely timbered 12,000-hectare property when they spotted half a dozen of their cows. They had unbranded calves with them – some of them looked around 18 months old and had probably never seen a human. 'If we didn't grab them then it could be another two years before we got another chance,' he told me.

They moved fast. Terry's dog Dan set off with his pup Oscar. Sam had to keep driving because he had somewhere to be, so Terry jumped out of the ute and followed the two dogs into the rough terrain, tracking them by their barks. He knew he had to get in and out quickly; he couldn't risk getting lost in the thick scrub in the dark. These two skilled dogs rounded up the small mob of belligerent cattle and got them back onto the road within half an hour.

With Sam and the ute gone, Terry started the seven-kilometre walk towards home. Along the way, the two dogs rounded up more cattle that had wandered up onto the road for the warmth of the gravel at night. Terry could hear them but couldn't see them. It didn't matter; he had absolute faith in the dogs. It was 9pm by the time an exhausted Terry walked into the cattle yards with 50 cows behind him, kept in line the entire way by Dan and Oscar.

'If it was any other dogs, I wouldn't have tried it, but I just knew that every beast we started with would still be there by the time we got home.' I could hear the pride in Terry's voice as he told me the story and I thanked him for sharing it. 'No,' he said. 'Thank you for letting me tell people how awesome those dogs were.'

EPILOGUE

On a Sunday morning in June 2023, in the middle-class Melbourne suburb of Elwood with its federation cottages and pretty gardens, 1300 sausage dogs went for a walk. It was a chaotic scene, with the yappy little dachshunds tugging at their leads, keen to set off on what would be a record-breaking adventure.

The Guinness Book of Records has long held its own record for the most weird and whacky challenges over the decades. When I was younger, I remember being thrilled to unwrap the children's version of the large hardcover book at Christmas time, marvelling at the lengths people would go to for their short moment of fame: world's fastest talker, heaviest train pulled with a beard, world's tallest cow, fastest marathon dressed as an elf, longest duration balancing on one foot, and so on.

The months spent writing this book and the searches I had done for facts, stories and people in the *Muster Dogs* world were clearly starting to have an impact on my social media algorithms because each day something would pop up about this approaching canine record challenge. The organisers wanted to get the greatest number of dogs of a single breed together for a walk. Each dog would have to be registered in the hour before the walk and then, as a group, they would set off along the foreshore of Port Phillip Bay. The record was held by beagle owners and set in Macclesfield, England, in 2018, where organisers rounded up 1029 of these pets.

The Melbourne event would feature only dachshunds – more commonly known as sausage dogs – and they had to be pure-bred. Finally, I thought to myself, these could be the 'Mustard Dogs' that people misheard me as saying when I'd first told them about the show I was working on. I shared a notice about the dachshund event on my social media accounts, and with my working dog kelpies and border collies in mind, commented in my post that these short-legged little canines might not be mustering much but it was bound to be an entertaining morning.

'Oh, they can muster alright!' one reader posted immediately.

'They muster quail, Lisa!' another responded with an exclamation mark to signify outrage at my ignorance.

Suddenly I had a deluge of dachshund defenders on my social media feed. Someone told me their brother's sausage dog was always mustering something out of the woodpile, and that they were the original badger hunters, despite their petiteness.

A dog owner called Lynn told me her two pooches ran every weekend at their local parkrun, a 5-kilometre community event held around the world every Saturday. She told me Sir Chutney Waddlesworth had racked up 70 parkruns. Lady Olive Waddlesworth, who was just seven months old, had only completed ten – still, it was quite an achievement. I had no choice but to close the laptop on a morning of writing and head to the park to witness this bunch of hopeful record-breakers myself.

The weather gods were shining on the organisers. There was a chilly winter breeze, but the sun was out and the small animals were well rugged up – some outlandishly so. One couple had squeezed their dog lengthwise into an outfit that made it look like it actually was the sausage in a bread roll. There was a higgledy-piggledy line that stretched as far as I could see, and one of the organisers could be heard over the scratchy speaker encouraging everyone to stay patient because without proper registration the Guinness World Records officials wouldn't accept the attempt.

A drone was piloted into the sky to capture this unusual sight from above and the organiser sang out to the crowd, 'Wave your sausages in the air like you just don't care! Wave your sausages in the air like you just don't care!' Of course, they did care – very much. But they followed the instructions, and in a move that would defeat the owners of most other breeds, except perhaps the chihuahua, 1300 sausage dogs were lifted high above heads and waved around.

Thousands of little feet then padded their way into the history books.

The record was broken, proud dog owners went off in search of coffee and I headed to a friend's house to debrief about the wonderful world of dogs I'd stepped into since that first phone call 18 months earlier asking me to narrate the *Muster Dogs* series.

I'm often asked why *Muster Dogs* became such a hit, not just with people in regional Australia who saw themselves reflected onscreen but with city slickers who'd never before pondered how a hundred head of cattle could be shifted with minimum fuss across long distances, or how reluctant goats or sheep could be rounded up by a few dogs and one person riding a horse or a bike.

The cast was a key element, of course. Viewers were fascinated by Frank, Joni, CJ, Aticia and Rob in the first series and then Steve, Lily, Zoe, Russ and Cilla in the second. And then there were the landscapes, the challenges, the kindness the participants exhibited and their vulnerability. But the dogs themselves were easily the stars of this new concept. To so many of us, dogs are more than best friends – they connect us to a time, a place, family and friends.

When I was ten, we moved from Kilkivan to Gympie, which felt like a metropolis in comparison. We lived in town, on a street with neighbours on either side, where newspapers were delivered with a thud on the driveway and an ice-cream truck arrived weekly, alerting us with its 'Greensleeves' soundtrack. I found reassurance in being able to see lights instead of darkness. Walking past other people's houses, we got a peek inside loungerooms with families sprawled on couches, eyes focused on the flickering light of a television.

I made a new friend at school – Amanda – who lived with her sister and parents on a farm 40 kilometres from Gympie. They had about 100 dairy cows, including Jersey cows that had been my mum's favourite because of their 'pretty faces'. Amanda's parents would milk 80 cattle twice a day and had what you called 'Herringbone' bales where the cows enter and back themselves into stalls on either side of a pit. Whoever did the milking would stand in the pit dug lower than the cows, so that their hooves were at waist height. There'd be six cows on either side – and while one side was being milked, you'd be prepping and washing the udders on the other side to get ready to make the switch. Amanda's dad would often do the milking by himself, and it was fascinating to watch. I didn't realise it at the time, but both of her parents had jobs off the farm on top of being primary producers.

Those weekends spent at Amanda's place were special. Her mum would always make a fudge-like biscuit that was so memorable that 35 years later I asked Amanda if she still had the recipe. She sent me a photo of a page from a spiral-bound notepad in writing that was familiar from school. At the top of the page, above all the glorious ingredients of brown sugar and butter and choc bits and walnut, and the greasy signs of a recipe well used, was its name: 'Mum's Slice'.

It took an hour on the bus from the high school to the farm, and there'd still be a few chores waiting on our arrival. Amanda's least favourite duty was feeding the chooks. She'd have a bucket with vegetable scraps and rather than go into the chook pen with the hungry pecking birds, she'd fling it over the fence. It only delayed the inevitable; she had to venture in there at some point, once her mum had run out of buckets, but I squibbed it and stayed outside. If I was lucky, I'd be allowed to do some ear tagging on the calves with Amanda's dad, who teased me that he could pierce my ear too at the same time if I was keen. I was not.

The dogs were always with us. Over the years there was Katrina, Angie, Brutus, Tonto and Cleo – and while Cleo was a labrador and not a working dog, she was still an integral part of Amanda's family dynamic. Dogs – they're always connecting us to family, friends and place.

It's difficult to calculate how many dogs have joined previously animal-free households since the pandemic kept so many of us at home, but wander along to an off-leash park and you get a sense of the surge in dog ownership. I spoke to several councils whose boundaries take in the urban sprawl of our big cities. They're all preparing for a growing population. The size of the residential blocks are getting smaller, but the houses are getting bigger. That means planning for more green space and more dog parks. The local government on the Northern Beaches of Sydney told me that the number of microchipped dogs in their area had increased in the five years since 2018 by almost 16,000 to a total of 70,000.

One wintry weekend, just a few blocks from my home in inner Melbourne, I watched an instructor take a dozen dogs and their owners through their paces. He pulled orange cones out of the back of his car and set up what appeared to be an obstacle course with jumps. Confident owners, with their mix of tiny dogs, big dogs and breeds I couldn't begin to name, arrived with their scarves wrapped around their necks and beanies pulled down tight.

I saw a burly bearded man with two small matching white dogs, one of whom was called Chilli. I know that because he was wearing a hooded sweater with their photos printed on the back, along with the words: 'This human is owned by Chilli and ...' The other name was obscured, and I didn't want to interrupt his concentration, so I never discovered the name of Chilli's four-footed partner. Dog schools are in high demand and some of the lessons they offer sound similar to the routines our Muster Dogs went through. They're taught to sit and stay, come back to their owners when called, and learn to do that without distraction, as well as 'loose lead' walking and many of the tasks tackled by country working dogs.

My friend Vicki took her West Highland terrier to puppy school and I was keen to find out how it went. Esther is one of the most loved – and most indulged – dogs I know. 'We had to leave before she was expelled because she was so disruptive,' Vicki told me. 'She just wanted to play.' I was hardly surprised that the now-four-year-old Esther wasn't interested in taking instructions. I asked Vicki if I could write about her in this book and reassured her that I could change both her and Esther's names to prevent any embarrassment, but Vicki insisted I needn't bother. She wasn't at all sheepish that she doted on her dog just as she would a spoilt child. Her partner, Adam, was a little more abashed as I took up my position on the couch with a glass of wine to witness their night-time routine.

Esther has 52 toys in a basket and each night shortly after dinner, with her little white ears erect and her tail wagging, she'll offer up a cry that means she's ready to have the basket tipped over. She's then able to choose the toy of her liking for that evening's playtime. The night I'm there she chooses a green disc called Frisbee. I'm told that's a rare choice because normally it's Itchy the flea, Kitty the cat, Mia the meercat or Giovanna the giraffe. Adam sits at one end of the hallway and Vicki at the other and then this couple in their fifties toss the toy back and forth along the polished wooden floors for Esther to scurry after. She decides when the game ends and then she begins preparing for bed.

There are several padded areas to settle down on, with a toy on each, but you won't be surprised to know Esther would rather sleep with her owners. They've upgraded to a king-size bed because 'Esther likes to sleep horizontally'. I tell them, with the warmth of a close friendship, that they're two of the worst enablers of bad pet behaviour I've ever met. 'I know you said "two", but I oppose a lot!' Adam insisted.

I popped in to see them because, despite owning a dog that refused to come when called – a dog they feared would run onto the road and didn't trust to leave with anyone for a night, let alone a weekend, a dog they didn't believe in chastising or containing – they were avid *Muster Dogs* viewers. They'd been fascinated with the working dogs of Australia and how they'd been trained. 'I know I have to be better with Esther,' Vicki lamented.

I didn't have the heart to tell her I thought Esther was a lost cause. But I did want to understand why a couple of city dwellers, with a pampered pooch, felt as attached to the program as the people whose lives were being portrayed on the show. Why had *Muster Dogs* had such a huge cultural impact? Why did it appeal across a range of generations and locations and diversity of audiences?

There was the obvious reason, that it allowed people to travel vicariously after several years of pandemic lockdown. And it was a great show, which treated the audience and its participants with respect. It didn't mean there weren't uncomfortable moments for some viewers who were unfamiliar with the rough and tumble of country life. Vicki still struggled with seeing dogs in cages onscreen, despite the assurances I passed on from Frank that the cages, up high, with tight fencing wire, kept working dogs safe from snakes. I also relayed to them what all our *Muster Dogs* participants had told me – that the urge to 'work' is so strong that if the dogs aren't caged at night they'll head off looking for livestock and could end up being injured, hit by cars or lost.

'Oh, I could never do that to Esther,' Vicki remarked, as her dog nestled into her lap, having just moments ago reversed into Vicki's shins to alert her that she needed to be elevated from the floor. I left them to their night-time wind-down and strolled home.

I'd learned a lot myself since becoming immersed in the *Muster Dogs* world. Now the participants felt like friends, and I couldn't wait to follow their lives with their new and old four-legged pals. I asked producer Monica what her favourite moments were, but she confessed she was still putting final touches to the edit and her anxiety levels were too high to relax and reflect.

'The journey isn't over for me because I want everyone to feel like they're being seen and heard and represented respectfully,' she told me. 'I'm so grateful that they've trusted us to share their story.'

The show connects people in the dog park over a yarn, and it's connected disparate regional communities over discussions about the livestock industry. It connects city and country people as a feel-good, safe conversation starter. 'Another show that someone is watching could be polarising for somebody else, and you can't talk about it without it becoming an argument, but *Muster Dogs* connects people and just feels good,' Monica explained.

Muster Dogs also worked because our participants, from all parts of Australia, were prepared to show their vulnerabilities onscreen, despite the pressure of knowing that millions of people would be watching. You could feel their honesty. At the heart of all their efforts was a desire to tell the stories of regional Australia and to bridge a gap they felt had been widening as Australia's population migrated to the cities.

'I think *Muster Dogs* is a catalyst; it's a change maker,' Cilla told me on that last evening at the Clermont pub with the team. 'It's showing farmers and rural people in their true light, the genuine people that they are, as innovators, as intelligent and gorgeous people who are being reminded as well that if they put in the effort to do things the right way, it's rewarded and there's status in that.'

We're not blind to the fact that there are people who haven't adopted Frank's plea to treat their animals with kindness. Tess, the vet in Clermont, sees some of that mistreatment still, but much less than when she first joined her father in the clinic 20-odd years ago. There's an acknowledgement among even the hardest of stockmen and women that these dogs are not only workers but companions.

Over the past two decades, Tess has witnessed farmers and musterers who wouldn't have spent hard-earned money on veterinary bills in the past now begging her for help. She's convinced that *Muster Dogs* has helped remove some of the guilt. 'I think it's a hangover from generations of austerity where farmers felt they couldn't spend money on animals,' she told me. 'But I've definitely noticed a shift. It's like they've been given permission, and I'm certainly not going to tell anyone down at the pub that you just dropped four grand trying to save your dog.'

These beautiful, playful, talented, goofy dogs have kept us all transfixed. Jerry, our sound recordist, learned a lot getting to know the participants, watching the training and understanding the psychology. It was a privilege, he told me. 'This is the job we do, just like their job is to work their dogs – but it's such a pleasure when the subject is as beautiful. I mean, what an office!'

Producer Sally Browning will always remember having a front-row seat to the blooming relationship between a trainer and their dog. 'It was a beautiful thing,' she told me from Bali where she was having her first few days off from *Muster Dogs* duties. 'There are people here at the retreat who can't stop talking about how they would get together with their friends and watch it each Sunday night and felt such a connection with the characters.' Sally wasn't missing some of the basic accommodation in the outback that had been home for days on end during some of the shoots. 'But then, when I look at the rushes [raw footage], it always makes me nostalgic to be back with the dust, dogs and the big hats in the relentless sun.'

For producer Michael Boughen, a city boy living in the country, the project has filled his life with joy. 'I'd love people to understand what happens in country life. There can be a bit of a jaundiced view, but people in the country get up in the morning, have a cup of coffee, put their pants on and go to work like the rest of us.'

The participants of series one have all been affected by their involvement. Life on CJ's property is busier since she appeared on the show. She and Joe took on more trade cattle, which is the cattle-type they buy as weaners and then bulk up to sell seven or eight months later. CJ has been putting together livestock and working dog schools and hopes to get Joni, who she bonded with through the *Muster Dogs* experience, to the Top End soon. And she has also discovered on school visits how much of a rockstar Spice is, and how much schoolkids love the show. 'I wasn't just hearing from our local kids how they loved it; I was visiting schools in town and they were coming up and recognised us and just loved it, which was great.'

CJ is grateful for the women who've gone before her who made being a female grazier easier, as well as the network she has around her. She doesn't think of herself as being isolated, not like some women on the land. She's passionate about the role women play, and after *Muster Dogs* she graduated from the inaugural LeadHer program run by Australian Women in Agriculture. Thanks to her decision to join the cast, her voice on important issues is now louder.

Rob knows he's lucky to be in a financial position to have been able to spend time on the show, with so many other farmers under a mountain of debt and having to concentrate on trying to turn a profit on their properties rather than deal with cameras. He reckons *Muster Dogs* did more good for the public's view of life on the land than any PR campaign over the last decade.

He is recognised more often now in the city and in larger regional centres, and fans of the show often strike up conversations. 'They'll check I'm Lucifer's dad and then they'll start telling me about their dog; they'll always have a story about their own dog,' he says with a laugh. The participants all understand it wasn't them but the dogs that were the stars of the show. 'Oh, we're just the supporting cast, we know that,' Rob says. 'Those dogs are the stars.'

Lucifer is happy working alongside Annie up at Hillview. With his new life came a name change. He's now known as Luci and is on his best manners when he visits aged care homes. He knocks his energy levels down a few gears: the more elderly the person he's meeting, the steadier the gaze he offers them. 'The older he gets, the better he'll be and that's exactly what's happening,' Frank says.

After *Muster Dogs* went to air, Aticia and her partner, Adam, thought about leaving Glenflorrie Station for a stint and maybe working their way around Australia with the dogs. But a surprise changed those plans. In July 2023, their daughter was born. They still decided to leave the station, where Aticia had lived since she was five, but instead of travelling they settled closer to their wider family, two and a half hours southeast of Perth. 'I think if we weren't looking for a break away from the station, I would have had Savannah there,' she says, 'although the isolation would have been stressful as a first-time mum with a newborn.'

Gossip moved too. In fact, Aticia took all her dogs from Glenflorrie Station, with a couple going to friends and seven remaining with her. She loves receiving messages from kelpie owners who feel they understand their dogs more thanks to that first series. 'I felt like kelpies were underappreciated, and for people who had them, I was hoping they would look at their dogs and go, "You know what? These dogs actually do so much for me and they deserve to be treated really well." And that was my main reason for doing the show.'

Joni's solitary life on the road with her 20 dogs in a truck, going wherever the work took her, was spellbinding for viewers. The logistics of it alone were startling: 60 kilos of food a week, 30 litres of water a day. She'd start her day around 3.45am on invoices and bookwork and would fuel up on caffeine before getting the dogs out.

When this tough cattle educator gave us a glimpse of her private thoughts in series one and admitted it was a lonely life, we wanted to give her a collective hug. This was a woman who would spend weeks without seeing another person. Cracking jokes was her way of deflecting the hard questions. But just once, in front of the cameras, she allowed us into her world, admitting it was sometimes tough.

Joni's never really got used to being recognised, especially in the outback when she's least expecting it. 'If I'm in my truck in my cowgirl gear, I can't drive anywhere without people wanting to say g'day,' she says. 'I was pulled up in Willare, which is basically one roadhouse in the middle of nowhere, and they were getting Chet out to take a photo.'

She's still working for clients – some of them the biggest names in grazing in this country. And she also still sets up camp with an eye out for crocodiles. 'I've got to set up site away from any crocs because when it's really hot, like

44 degrees, those dogs will just take off for a swim no matter how good I'm calling them.'

Like all the other participants, Joni's world has been changed by being part of the *Muster Dogs* caravanserai. She's a household name now, as well as a solitary, self-reliant and courageous character working in one of the most stark and challenging corners of the world. Only now, she also has the eyes of the world on her.

And as for the dogs we've come to know so well, their lives have become part of a national conversation. Annie, now a big star, travels far and wide, admired in the city and the country as a 'lovely dog'. And Buddy will no doubt follow in her footsteps, under Zoe's watchful eye, after becoming the second pup to earn the title of champion Muster Dog.

No matter where we are watching *Muster Dogs*, whether it is in our inner-city homes or out on big sprawling properties, we have grown to admire and respect these incredible dogs. They are all champions to us. Skilled, smart and seemingly tireless, they skip across the backs of sheep and jump up onto four-wheelers, eager to get to work. They will keep bringing home the herds – the cattle and the sheep – proving their worth as a treasured part of a long Australian tradition. And we will continue to watch on with awe.

Sources

Prologue

Muster Dogs *is simply delightful TV as well as being thoughtful, engaged and cast with a bunch of wonderful characters*: Graeme Blundell, 'Muster Pups and Outback Ringer brilliant Australian Television', *Weekend Australian*, 21 January 2022.

Chapter 3:

Definition of 'sparrow's fart': Paul Anthony Jones's post on 'sparrowfart' in his blog Haggard Hawks (www.haggardhawks.com/post/sparrowfarts, 1 November 2017) led me to this dictionary: A Native of Craven, *The Dialect of Craven*, vol.II, W.M. Crofts, 1828, London.

Many of us now use food as a marker for our values: carnivore, vegan, vegetarian, pescatarian, gluten-free, paleo ...: Gabrielle Chan, *Why You Should Give a F*ck About Farming*, Vintage Australia, 2021, p.18.

Chapter 4

Breeder, trainer and historian Nancy Withers tells the story of a young Irish bloke called Jack Gleeson ...: Sandy Guy, 'Kelpie Country', *Australian Geographic* magazine, May–June 2023.

University of Sydney study on interbreeding between kelpies and dingoes: Tracy Chew, Cali E. Willet, Bianca Haase & Claire M. Wade, 'Genomic Characterization of External Morphology Traits in Kelpies Does Not Support Common Ancestry with the Australian Dingo', *Genes* 2019, 10(5), 337.

Acknowledgements

The last time I owned a dog was 30 years ago when an old boyfriend rescued a mutt called Baxter. He was not the happiest of dogs, which I only realised later was most likely the result of how he'd been treated before we adopted him. Still, he was ours and we loved him.

What a difference kindness and respect can make to an animal's life.

Thank you to the wonderful participants and trainers and breeders who showed me that again and again. To Frank, CJ, Aticia, Joni, Rob, Russ, Cilla, Zoe, Lily, Steve, Keri, Helen, Neil, Mick, Carolyn and Joe and all their families – you invited me into your homes and lives; you took my calls at all hours of the day and night; you even drew pictures of mobs of livestock and texted them to me to try to help me understand what a dog was doing. I am so grateful.

This book would not exist without *Muster Dogs* producer Monica O'Brien who had faith in this project (and in me) from the beginning and delivered words of encouragement and support on a daily basis during the long days of writing. I don't know where she gets her energy or capacity to juggle so many projects at the one time but she always seemed to find time for me. Thank you for your friendship, Mon. And thank you to Michael Boughen, whose confidence that I could deliver something worthy of the *Muster Dogs* brand helped buoy me during moments of self-doubt.

The entire team at Ambience Entertainment – led by Matthew Street – helped bring this beautiful gift that is the *Muster Dogs* TV series into the world and I will always be grateful I was asked along for the ride. To the camera, sound and editing crews who shared their stories with me for this book – thank you. None of it would have happened without my colleagues at the ABC who took a punt on this show and then backed this book. Jo and Rachel in particular – thank you.

And to my workmates at *News Breakfast*, who I am also lucky enough to call my friends, thank you for letting me bang on about this book for so long – even when the stories of the latest challenge I might have been facing would start in the newsroom before 4am!

To my oldest friends who let me tell their stories and especially my family, who never tired of retelling details of life on the farm in Kilkivan – thank you for not losing your patience with the constant pings of the messaging app. You'd be forgiven if you muted me!

This book is a team effort and wouldn't be in the shape it is without editor Madeleine James and publisher Mary Rennie who brought new ideas and great suggestions to every conversation we had.

I have been incredibly lucky over the years to be able to call the whip-smart Pamela Williams a friend and mentor. She lingered over every word in this manuscript, always finding ways to make it a better version than the one I handed to her. Pam – thank you for caring about the *Muster Dogs* family and their stories as much as me.

And finally, a note about a dog called Alfie – a stumpy-tail cattle dog who belonged to my nephew Chris. He patiently posed for photos with me for social media and would stick his nose into my room when I visited to see what I was up to. My sister Wendy doted on Alfie, tending to his ailments late in his life with the dedication of an emergency-room nurse. Alfie died while I was writing this book and the hole that he left for those who loved him reminded me of the intense emotional connections we have with dogs. They can be co-workers or just companions. Either way they should be cherished by those lucky enough to have them in their lives.